The Grammar of Spelling

GRADE 6

The Grammar of Spelling

GRADE 6

Matt Whitling

Published by Logos Press
The Curriculum Division of Canon Press
PO Box 8729, Moscow, Idaho 83843
800-488-2034 | www.logospressonline.com

Matt Whitling, *The Grammar of Spelling, Grade 6*

Cover design & illustration by Forrest Dickison
Interior design by Valerie Anne Bost

23 24 25 26 27 28 29 30 31 32 10 9 8 7 6 5 4 3 2

Contents

The Art of Reading and Writing English . . . 1

Sixth Grade Spelling . . . 3

Lesson Features . . . 5

How to Use This Curriculum . . . 11

1 Rule #1, the Doubler . . . 15

2 Rule #2, Final ***e*** . . . 21

3 Rule #3, ***i*** before ***e*** . . . 27

4 Rule #4, Final ***y*** . . . 33

5 Rule #5, ***-ness/-ly*** . . . 39

6 Prefixes . . . 45

7 Prefixes . . . 51

8 Prefixes . . . 57

9 Spelling Goblins . . . 63

10 Stumpers . . . 67

11 Stumpers . . . 71

12 Stumpers . . . 75

13 Science . . . 81

14 Review Stumpers . . . 87

15 Review Stumpers . . . 93

16 Science, American History . . . 97

17 Math, World War II . . . 101

18 Science, Stumpers 105

19 Stumpers 109

20 History 113

21 Stumpers 117

22 Geometry, History 121

23 Stumpers 125

24 Stumpers 129

25 Stumpers 133

26 Stumpers Review 137

27 Stumpers Review 141

28 Science, History 145

29 Stumpers 149

30 Science, History 153

31 Stumpers 157

32 History, Stumpers 161

33 Stumpers 165

34 Review 169

35 Review 173

36 Science 177

Master List of Spelling Words 183

Master List of Spelling Rules 191

Blank Worksheets 193

The Art of Reading and Writing English

ISAAC WATTS

The knowledge of letters is one of the greatest blessings that ever God bestowed on the children of men. By this means we preserve for our own use, through all our lives, what our memory would have lost in a few days, and lay up rich treasure of knowledge for those that shall come after us.

By the arts of reading and writing, we can sit at home and acquaint ourselves with what is done in all the distant parts of the world, and find what our fathers did long ago in the first ages of mankind. By this means a Briton holds correspondence with his friend in America or Japan, and manages all his traffic. We learn by this means how the old Romans lived, how the Jews worshiped: We learn what Moses wrote, what Enoch prophesied, where Adam dwelt, and what he did soon after the creation; and those who shall live when the Day of Judgement comes, may learn by the same means what we now speak, and what we do in Great Britain, or in the land of China.

In short, the art of letters does, as it were, revive all the past ages of men, and set them at once upon the stage; and brings all the nations from afar, and gives them, as it were, a general interview: so that the most distant nations, and distant ages of mankind may converse together, and grow into acquaintance.

But the greatest blessing of all, is the knowledge of the Holy Scripture, wherein God has appointed his servants in ancient times to write down the discoveries which he has made of his power and justice, His providence and grace, that we who live near the end of time may learn the way to heaven and everlasting happiness.

Thus letters give us a sort of immortality in this world, and they are given us in the Word of God to support our immortal hopes in the next.

Those therefore who willfully neglect this sort of knowledge, and despise the art of letters, need no heavier curse of punishment than what they choose for themselves, to live and die in ignorance both of the things of God and man.

If the terror of such a thought, will not awaken the slothful to seek so much acquaintance with their mother-tongue, as may render them capable of some of the advantages here described; I know not where to find a persuasive that shall work upon souls, that are sunk down so far into brutal stupidity, and so unworthy of a reasonable nature.

Sixth Grade Spelling

Children in the Grammar stage love knowledge and facts. They are fascinated by words, and they can memorize easily. Spelling correctly is a "tool" we want to give the students that will help them with written communication.

Spelling is a discipline. It is hard work. This spelling program lacks pretty pictures and the fluff of other programs on the market. The no-nonsense worksheets that accompany each lesson are basically an exercise in rewriting the spelling words many times. Spelling, for the sixth grade student, concentrates on hearing each part of the basic root word. The student works primarily with a foundation, using the building blocks of reading and phonics. However, this approach is not a reading-spelling program with twenty-nine or thirty spelling or phonics rules for the students to memorize. It is a program of hearing blends, clusters and vowel sounds, memorizing words, and being able to spell dictated words and sentences. The emphasis is on the *words themselves*. The strength of this spelling program is the cumulative spelling lists and dictation.

Word Lists for the Sixth Grade

1. Words that follow simple spelling rules (***i*** before ***e*** except after ***c***, etc.)
2. Terms relating to other school subjects (math, science, history, Bible, etc.)
3. Common prefixes and suffixes added to base words (*uni-*, *tri-*, *co-*, etc.)
4. Lots and lots of stumpers, including some particularly challenging "spelling goblins."

Lesson Features

The thirty-six lessons in *The Grammar of Spelling, Grade 6* provide a full year's curriculum. Each lesson includes instruction, practice, and a test to measure mastery.

Word Boxes

Each lesson's spelling words appear in a Word Box. These may be copied and sent home each week for study purposes.

The words are taught by a cumulative method. Each week the students are given a word box containing twenty to twenty-five new words. Review words are noted. These words may show up on the spelling test, so the students need to remember how to spell them.

Lessons

Information is given about each lesson and instructions on what to teach are presented. Introduce the new spelling words and discuss the meaning of those words. Demonstrate family relationships, if possible. Emphasize hearing each sound in words. Orally discuss exceptions, sight words, meaning of homophones, and the adding of prefixes and suffixes.

Extra Words based on Logos Press homeschool bundles are provided for dictation and practice. These words can be used for whole class or individual instruction.

Worksheets

Help the students identify the particular pattern or patterns for each week's words. The worksheets have four main parts:

1. **Repeat and Write**: In this activity the teacher says the spelling word, the students listen, repeat the word in unison, and then write the word on the blank in print.

2. **Alphabetize in Print**: The students are to alphabetize the words in groups and then print the words in the blanks. If they write the alphabetized number in the small circle provided and copy the words only after the entire list is numbered, mistakes can be corrected easily. For example, in Lesson 1 the students are to find the word that comes first alphabetically. This word is *batting*. Therefore, in the circle to the right of the word *batting*, the student is to write the number 1. The number 2 will be written in the circle following the word *blower* and so forth. This activity should be done together as a whole class led by the teacher for the first few weeks until the students understand how to alphabetize using the circles correctly.
3. **Flip and Write**: The students will look carefully at the word on Worksheet A, keep the spelling in mind, flip to Worksheet B, and write the word in print or cursive as instructed by you. Do not allow the students to fold their papers and copy without flipping.
4. **Cursive**: The students are to carefully and neatly print each spelling word in cursive. This provides an opportunity to see the words in a different format than usual, requiring more care and checking to ensure that the words are indeed spelled correctly.

Blank worksheets are available in the back of the book for teachers who want to create their own. These can be particularly helpful for reviewing words your students have struggled with.

Dictation

Cumulative spelling lists and dictation are the heart of this spelling program. Dictation helps the students hear and write sentences. It reinforces listening and following directions skills. Words and sentences are provided for practice during the week and for the weekly test.

Each sentence should be dictated as you have the students' undivided attention. Say the sentence; repeat the sentence. Have the students repeat the sentence back twice. Dictate the sentence once more, and then the students may write it. Allow enough time for them to write the sentence. Finally, dictate the sentence again so they may check their work. Proper capitalization and punctuation should be required and graded whenever the students write a sentence.

The teacher may need to spell some of the words in the sentences for the students.

Tests

Students will write tests on blank lined paper. See the next page for a sample test page. Students should do the following:

- Fold their papers in half lengthwise and reopen the paper.
- Write on every other line.
- Write *Spelling Test* as the title on the left-hand side.
- Write their name and the date on the right-hand side.
- Number their papers 1–13 along the left margin and 14–25 along the middle fold line. They should do this every week, no matter how many words are used for the test.
- Write their name again on the back at the top of the right-hand column.
- Numbers for dictated sentences will be written later as needed.

When giving the test, state the number and the word. Give a sentence using the word. Repeat the word one time only. Give the students ample time to write and then move on to the next word. Do not go back over the words. The students can and must learn to listen and spell promptly.

After giving the spelling words, have the students write the two sentences you dictate to them. Follow the same procedure for the test as you did during the practice lesson. (See the above directions.)

Each word on the test paper must be spelled correctly. Capitals and punctuation in sentences count equal to spelling words. (That's integration!) It is for you to decide to take off full or partial credit if a student fails to cross *t*'s and dot *i*'s and *j*'s.

Sample Test Sheet, Page 1

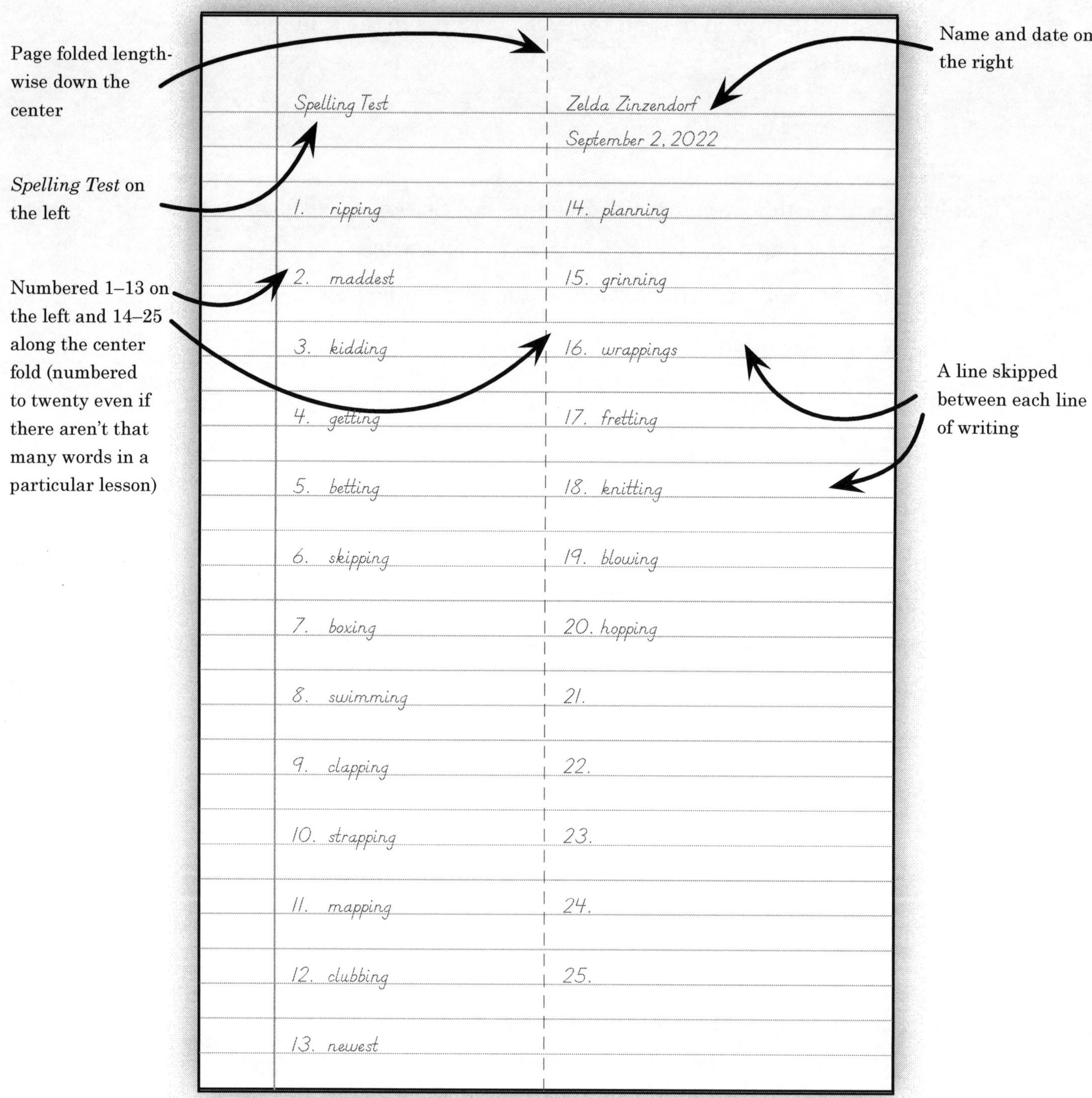

Sample Test Sheet, Page 2

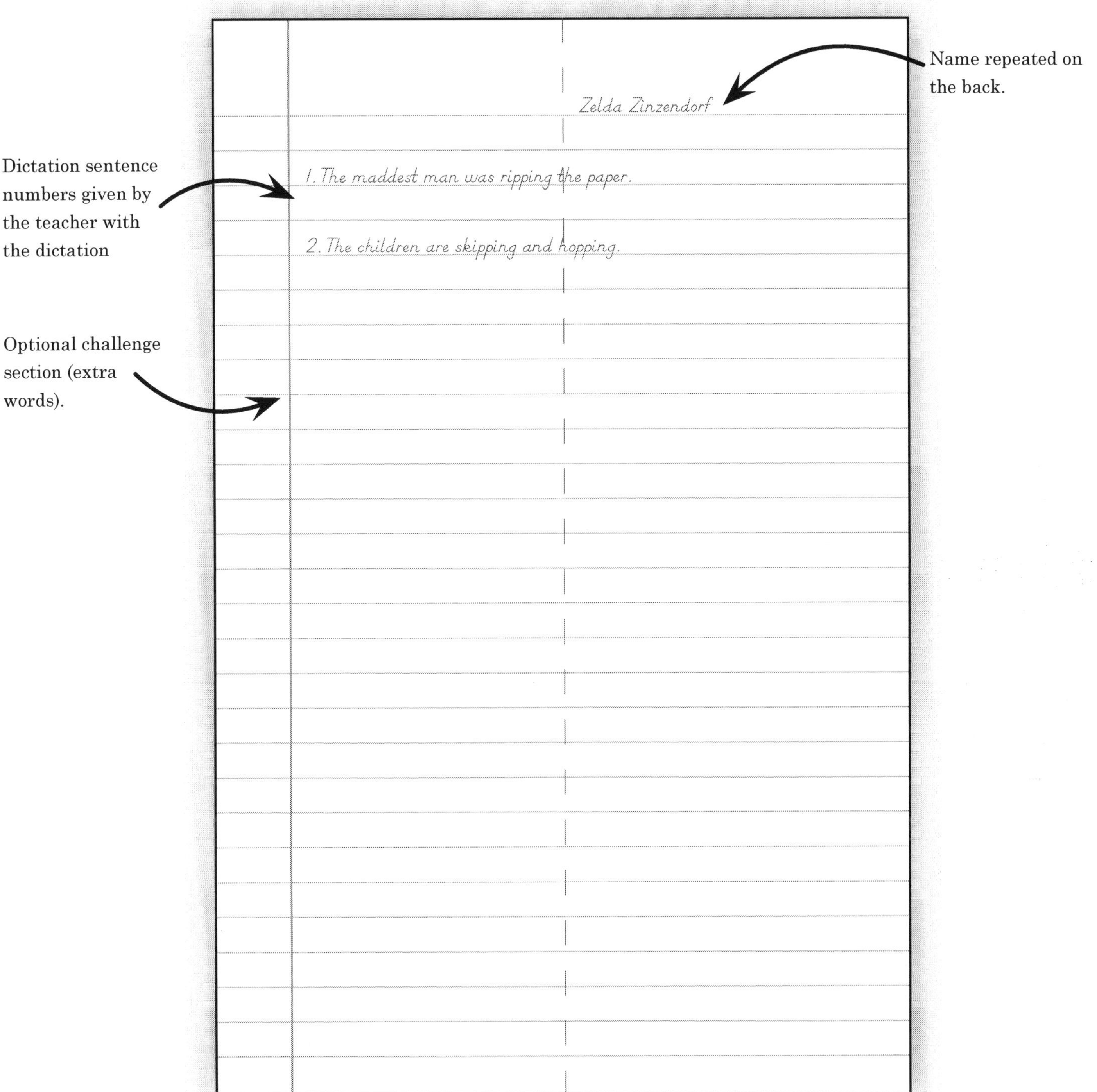

How to Use This Curriculum

Homework

Word Boxes: Send the new and review word boxes home on Monday or the previous Friday.

Monday (30 minutes)

Preview Time: Introduce the new spelling words and discuss the meaning of those words. Demonstrate family relationships, if possible. Emphasize *hearing* each sound in the word. Orally discuss exceptions, sight words, meanings of homophones, and the adding of prefixes and suffixes. This preview time will be as exciting and interesting to the students as you make it.

Worksheet A: Using the left column of the worksheet dictate each word to the students. They are to listen, repeat the word in unison, and then print the word on the blank. Using the right column, have students alphabetize each group of words. A few worksheets have additional exercises.

Tuesday (30 minutes)

Worksheet B: Have students flip back to Worksheet A, look at the first word, then flip back to Worhsheet B and write it in the left column. Repeat for each word. Tell the students whether you want them to use print or cursive. In the right column, have them rewrite each word in cursive. If you are using the extra words, have students complete that section according to the same instructions as Worksheet A.

Wednesday (30 minutes)

Dictation: Dictate words from the new spelling list, from the extra words provided with each lesson.

Worksheets: The students may complete the worksheets, if they haven't done so yet.

Thursday and Friday (30 minutes each)

Testing: Give two spelling tests each week and record test scores for both. If a student gets 100% on Thursday, he does not have to take Friday's test and gets an automatic 100% for it. Students love this reward for hard work and a job well done. Usually the grades drastically improve for the second test. Friday's test does not have to be the same words. You, as the teacher, may want to change the test words.

Integration

Using the "tool": Expect and require the students to apply correct spelling to their other work as well. Require them to copy correctly. Challenge the students who get 100% three times in a row by adding some or all of the Extra Words to their spelling test. They can write these on the back after the dictation sentences.

Extra Words

If you are using the extra words in each lesson, have students practice them on Worksheet B.

Parents who are using the Logos Press homeschool bundles may enjoy adding a few words to each week that are connected with what students are learning in other subjects. In particular, they are taken from *Covenantal Catechism 5*, *Noeo Science: Chemistry 2*, and Logos Press reading guides. We have provided five extra words each week. There are none for lessons 37 and on, because the bundles only have 36 weeks' worth of words.

Lesson 1: elastic, watts, joules, members, doldrums

Lesson 2: pendulum, fibers, trampoline, perilous, infinity

Lesson 3: convection, conduction, radiation, religion, conjunctions

Lesson 4: fission, equilibrium, fulcrum, ceremonial, immediately

Lesson 5: inertia, momentum, office-bearer, second coming, campaign

Lesson 6: lubricant, friction, resistance, sovereign, truce

Lesson 7: velocity, acceleration, collision, Galatia, throng

Lesson 8: centripetal, unstable, divisions, Corinth, reek

Lesson 9: ramp, liberty, idolatry, cram, carrion

Lesson 10: symmetrical, balancing point, seesaw, tongues, variation

Lesson 11: gear, pulley, wedge, firstfruits, nihilist

Lesson 12: density, Archimedes, Hiero, heathen, lubber

Lesson 13: Euclid, mechanics, engine, propitiation, extricate

Lesson 14: eureka, buoyancy, cosmos, justification, doornail

Lesson 15: pi, indeterminate, approximate, imputation, catechism

Lesson 16: hydrofoils, submarines, baptism, penalty, voracious

Lesson 17: Bernoulli's principle, pitch, yaw, instrument, embassies

Lesson 18: combustion, suspension, transmission, mortify, dexterously

Lesson 19: frequency, amplitude, transverse, jesting, thane

Lesson 20: luminous, translucent, opaque, substance, apparition,

Lesson 21: diffraction, incandescence, luminescence, edifying, apothecary

Lesson 22: convex, concave, periscope, Melchizedek, melancholy

Lesson 23: Ptolemy, Aristotle, pendulum, priesthood, sumptuous

Lesson 24: Copernicus, Tycho, Kepler, mediator, discoursing

Lesson 25: Bellarmine, Barberini, heliocentric, revelation, unrequited

Lesson 26: nebula, asterism, elliptical, martyr, drought

Lesson 27: constellation, Ursa Major, Babylon, dholes, mohwa tree

Lesson 28: fusion, asteroid, comet, millennium, warren

Lesson 29: meteoroid, meteorite, dwarf planet, gossamer, knoll

Lesson 30: insulator, static, current, flotsam, bivouac

Lesson 31: circuit, conductor, precipitously, satiated, impertinent

Lesson 32: valence electron, delegation, contrite, ardently, reprieve

Lesson 33: iron, filings, magnetosphere, zinc, domains

Lesson 34: dipole, armature, commutator, temporary, motor

Lesson 35: generator, repel, attract, charge, Van de Graaff

Lesson 36: comb, electroscope, paperclip, foil, hover

Lesson 1

WORD BOX

Pattern—Rule #1, the Doubler: wrapping, dropping, batting, glowing, splattering, maddening, snapping, saddening, trappings, swimmingly, fittingly, winnable, unflappable, knowable, blower, sowed, sewed, grinned, mugged, slipperiest

Directions

The student should be able to spell his/her *first and last name* and put it on each test

Spelling and *test* are to be memorized and are required as headings on each spelling test paper throughout the year.

New Words: This year you will begin with the five rules from last year. Here is the first one: **If you have a single vowel word to add a vowel suffix to, double the lone consonant, but not with *x* or *w*.**

A single vowel word is a word with only one vowel: *pan, mad, flap.*

A vowel suffix is an ending that begins with a vowel: *-ing, -er, -ed.*

A lone consonant is the last letter in a single vowel word (There must be only one consonant at the end of the word. The only consonants that do not double are *x* and *w*): *pan, mad, flap.*

Introduce each word in the word box and explain how to spell it by stressing the syllables and the vowel sound. Rehearse the doubler rule often. Explain the meaning of each word.

Beginning with the first lesson, the students need to be reminded about how to put their spelling words in alphabetical order. They will be required to do it every week.

Extra Words

If you are using the extra words, have students practice them on Worksheet B.

- elastic
- watts
- joules
- members
- doldrums

Test 1 (39 points)

Heading (3 points)

At the top of the page, have students write *Spelling Test* (1 pt.) on the left and their full name (1 pt.) and the date (1 pt.) on the right. See pp. 8–9 for a sample test sheet.

Spelling Words (20 points)

† marks words that might need to be illustrated through example sentences such as these:

- Reginald reaped what he *sowed*.
- Sally *sewed* six seashells on her shirt sleeve.

1. splattering
2. unflappable
3. snapping
4. wrapping
5. fittingly
6. batting
7. grinned
8. winnable
9. knowable
10. slipperiest
11. dropping
12. trappings
13. sowed†
14. swimmingly
15. sewed†
16. glowing
17. mugged
18. maddening
19. saddening
20. blower

Dictation (16 points)

1. She was unflappable, so he grinned. (9 pts.)
2. The maddening dog was snapping. (7 pts.)

Worksheet 1A

Name: ______________________

Date: ______________________

What is the pattern? ______________________

Repeat and Write: Repeat each word aloud after your teacher. Then write the word carefully in **print**. Check the spelling and memorize how the letters fit together to make each word.

Alphabetize: Alphabetize the list in each group by numbering the bubbles that follow each word.

After you number all the bubbles, write the words in each group alphabetically in the right-hand column. **Print** your answers.

GROUP 1

Word	Write	Bubble	Alphabetized
1. wrapping	wrapping	6	1. batting
2. batting	batting	1	2. blower
3. winnable	winnable	5	3. dropping
4. blower	blower	2	4. trapping
5. trappings	trappings	4	5. winnable
6. dropping	dropping	3	6. wrapping

GROUP 1

Word	Write	Bubble	Alphabetized
1. splattering		○	1.
2. unflappable		○	2.
3. swimmingly		○	3.
4. fittingly		○	4.
5. glowing		○	5.
6. sowed		○	6.
7. sewed		○	7.

GROUP 3

1. snapping	________	◯	1. ________
2. knowable	________	◯	2. ________
3. grinned	________	◯	3. ________
4. slipperiest	________	◯	4. ________
5. saddening	________	◯	5. ________
6. mugged	________	◯	6. ________
7. maddening	________	◯	7. ________

Split the Words

Show how each word is made by splitting it into its parts. The first two are done for you.

1. wrapping	wrap + ing	11. glowing	________
2. batting	bat + ing	12. sowed	________
3. winnable	________	13. sewed	________
4. blower	________	14. snapping	________
5. trappings	________	15. knowable	________
6. dropping	________	16. grinned	________
7. splattering	________	17. slipperiest	________
8. unflappable	________	18. saddening	________
9. swimmingly	________	19. mugged	________
10. fittingly	________	20. maddening	________

Worksheet 1B

Name: ____________________

Date: ____________________

Flip and Write: Flip your paper over and look at the first spelling word. Flip the page back and write it in the left-hand column below. (Your teacher will tell you whether to use **print** or **cursive**.)

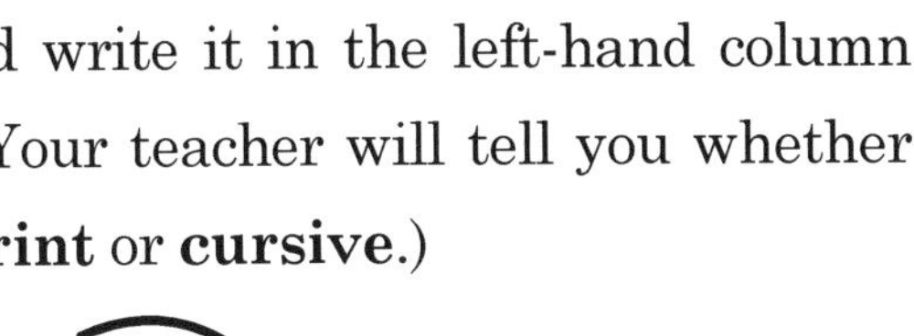

Cursive: Write the spelling words in cursive in the right-hand column below. Check each word to make sure you have written it correctly.

	Flip and Write		Cursive
1.	______	1.	______
2.	______	2.	______
3.	______	3.	______
4.	______	4.	______
5.	______	5.	______
6.	______	6.	______
7.	______	7.	______
8.	______	8.	______
9.	______	9.	______
10.	______	10.	______
11.	______	11.	______
12.	______	12.	______
13.	______	13.	______
14.	______	14.	______
15.	______	15.	______
16.	______	16.	______
17.	______	17.	______
18.	______	18.	______
19.	______	19.	______
20.	______	20.	______

Extra Words: Repeat and Write

1. elastic ______________________
2. watts ______________________
3. joules ______________________
4. members ______________________
5. doldrums ______________________

Alphabetize (Print)

1. ______________________
2. ______________________
3. ______________________
4. ______________________
5. ______________________

Review Rule #1, the Doubler

1. A single vowel word is a word with only one vowel: *pan, kid, clap*. These words have more than one vowel: *dream, dive, shape.*
2. A vowel suffix is a group of letters added to the end of a word that begins with a vowel: *-ed, -ing, -est, -ism*. These are consonant suffixes: *-ful, -ly, -ness, -hood.*
3. A lone consonant is a single consonant at the end of a word: *man, dog, pan*. These are not lone consonant words: *cake, dish, fill, soft.*

Lesson 2

WORD BOX

Pattern—Rule #2, Final *e*: safely, sincerely, speculation, immigration, participation, ignition, infiltrator, acknowledged, obligated, negotiated, influenced, irrigating, separating, hesitating, endorsement, amazement, requirement, noticeable, argument, awful

Directions

Review: Words from Lesson 1.

New Words: This week you review the second rule from last year: **For final *e* words remember this chant: a vowel suffix drops the *e*, a consonant suffix can't.**

A final *e* word is a word that ends with the letter *e*: *inflate, frustrate, safe*

A vowel suffix is an ending that begins with a vowel: *-ing, -ed, -er*

A consonant suffix is an ending that begins with a consonant: *-ly, -ful, -less*

Rehearse the final ***e*** rule often. Explain the meaning of each word.

Extra Words

If you are using the extra words, have students practice them on Worksheet B.

- pendulum
- fibers
- trampoline
- perilous
- infinity

Test 2 (43 points)

Heading (3 points)

Spelling Test (1 pt.), full name (1 pt.), date (1 pt.).

Spelling Words (25 points)

Review words are marked with an asterisk.

1. negotiated
2. acknowledged
3. infiltrator
4. ignition
5. safely
6. hesitating
7. requirement
8. irrigating
9. influenced
10. participation
11. endorsement
12. immigration
13. separating
14. argument
15. sincerely
16. noticeable
17. obligated
18. amazement
19. awful
20. speculation
21. dropping*
22. maddening*
23. batting*
24. glowing*
25. knowable*

Dictation (15 points)

1. He influenced the argument over immigration. (8 pts.)
2. He sincerely gave an endorsement. (7 pts.)

Worksheet 2A

Name: ______________________

Date: ______________________

What is the pattern? ______________________

Repeat and Write (Print)

GROUP 1

1. safely ______ ◯
2. speculation ______ ◯
3. infiltrator ______ ◯
4. acknowledged ______ ◯
5. irrigating ______ ◯
6. obligated ______ ◯

GROUP 2

1. separating ______ ◯
2. ignition ______ ◯
3. negotiated ______ ◯
4. sincerely ______ ◯
5. endorsement ______ ◯
6. amazement ______ ◯
7. hesitating ______ ◯

GROUP 3

1. noticeable ______ ◯
2. requirement ______ ◯
3. influenced ______ ◯
4. immigration ______ ◯
5. participation ______ ◯
6. argument* ______ ◯
7. awful* ______ ◯

Alphabetize (Print)

Group 1:

1. ______
2. ______
3. ______
4. ______
5. ______
6. ______

Group 2:

1. ______
2. ______
3. ______
4. ______
5. ______
6. ______
7. ______

Group 3:

1. ______
2. ______
3. ______
4. ______
5. ______
6. ______
7. ______

* There are quite a few deal breakers!

Split the Words

Show how each word is made by splitting it into its parts. The first two are done for you.

1. safely safe + ly
2. speculation speculate + tion
3. infiltrator ______
4. acknowledged ______
5. irrigating ______
6. obligated ______
7. separating ______
8. ignition ______
9. negotiated ______
10. sincerely ______
11. endorsement ______
12. amazement ______
13. hesitating ______
14. noticeable ______
15. requirement ______
16. influenced ______
17. immigration ______
18. participation ______
19. argument ______
20. awful ______

Worksheet 2B

Name: ____________________

Date: ____________________

Flip and Write

1. ____
2. ____
3. ____
4. ____
5. ____
6. ____
7. ____
8. ____
9. ____
10. ____
11. ____
12. ____
13. ____
14. ____
15. ____
16. ____
17. ____
18. ____
19. ____
20. ____

Cursive

1. ____
2. ____
3. ____
4. ____
5. ____
6. ____
7. ____
8. ____
9. ____
10. ____
11. ____
12. ____
13. ____
14. ____
15. ____
16. ____
17. ____
18. ____
19. ____
20. ____

Extra Words: Repeat and Write

1. pendulum ____
2. fibers ____
3. trampoline ____
4. perilous ____
5. infinity ____

Alphabetize (Print)

1. ____
2. ____
3. ____
4. ____
5. ____

Review Rule #2, Final *e*

1. A word that ends with an ***e*** is a final ***e*** word: *grate, bake, love*. These are not final ***e*** words: *fish, hook, guts*

2. A vowel suffix is a group of letters added to the end of a word that begin with a vowel: *-ed, -ing, -ist, -ism*. These are consonant suffixes: *-ful, -ly, -ness*.

   - When you add a vowel suffix to a final ***e*** word you must drop the ***e***.
   - When you add a consonant suffix to a final ***e*** word you keep the ***e***. (***y*** can act as a vowel or a consonant depending on the sound it makes.)

Lesson 3

WORD BOX

Pattern—Rule #3, *i* before *e*: feint, spontaneity, unveiled, altarpiece, conceitedly, briefing, neighborly, misconceive, overachieving, grief, chieftain, believability, deceitful, eighth, disbelief, diesel, unwieldy, underweight, counterfeit, height

Directions

Review: Words from lessons 1 and 2

New Words: This lesson has a rule from last year: ***i* before *e* except after *c*, or when sounded like *ā* as in *neighbor* and *weigh*.**

Introduce each word in the word box and explain how to spell it by stressing the syllables and the vowel sound. Rehearse the ***i*** before ***e*** rule often. Explain the meaning of each word.

Extra Words

If you are using the extra words, have students practice them on Worksheet B.

- convection
- conduction
- radiation
- religion
- conjunctions

Test 3 (45 points)

Heading (3 points)

Spelling Test (1 pt.), full name (1 pt.), date (1 pt.).

Spelling Words (25 points)

Review words are marked with an asterisk.

1. eighth
2. briefing
3. overachieving
4. unwieldy
5. counterfeit
6. grief
7. height
8. chieftain
9. neighborly
10. feint
11. altarpiece
12. spontaneity
13. believability
14. disbelief
15. underweight
16. deceitful
17. misconceive
18. conceitedly
19. diesel
20. unveiled
21. splattering*
22. maddening*
23. endorsement*
24. negotiated*
25. awful*

Dictation (17 points)

1. The deceitful chieftain made a feint. (8 pts.)
2. His maddening grief left me in disbelief. (9 pts.)

Worksheet 3A

Name: ____________________

Date: ____________________

What is the pattern? ____________________

Repeat and Write (Print) | **Alphabetize (Print)**

GROUP 1

1. feint ______ ◯ 1. ______
2. spontaneity ______ ◯ 2. ______
3. unveiled ______ ◯ 3. ______
4. altarpiece ______ ◯ 4. ______
5. conceitedly ______ ◯ 5. ______
6. misconceive ______ ◯ 6. ______

GROUP 2

1. neighborly ______ ◯ 1. ______
2. briefing ______ ◯ 2. ______
3. overachieving ______ ◯ 3. ______
4. grief ______ ◯ 4. ______
5. chieftain ______ ◯ 5. ______
6. believability ______ ◯ 6. ______
7. deceitful ______ ◯ 7. ______

GROUP 3

1. eighth ______ ◯ 1. ______
2. disbelief ______ ◯ 2. ______
3. diesel ______ ◯ 3. ______
4. unwieldy ______ ◯ 4. ______
5. underweight ______ ◯ 5. ______
6. counterfeit* ______ ◯ 6. ______
7. height* ______ ◯ 7. ______

* There are quite a few deal breakers!

Worksheet 3B

Name: ______________________

Date: ______________________

Flip and Write

1. ______
2. ______
3. ______
4. ______
5. ______
6. ______
7. ______
8. ______
9. ______
10. ______
11. ______
12. ______
13. ______
14. ______
15. ______
16. ______
17. ______
18. ______
19. ______
20. ______

Cursive

1. ______
2. ______
3. ______
4. ______
5. ______
6. ______
7. ______
8. ______
9. ______
10. ______
11. ______
12. ______
13. ______
14. ______
15. ______
16. ______
17. ______
18. ______
19. ______
20. ______

Extra Words: Repeat and Write

1. convection ______
2. conduction ______
3. radiation ______
4. religion ______
5. conjunctions ______

Alphabetize (Print)

1. ______
2. ______
3. ______
4. ______
5. ______

Review Rule #3, *i* before *e*

It is a common mistake for students to reverse the order of ***e*** and ***i*** in certain words.

1. If these two letters come after the letter ***c*** the ***e*** comes first (*ceiling*).

2. If they do not come after the letter ***c*** the ***i*** comes first (*brief*).

3. If they make the long ***ā*** sound the ***e*** comes first (*weigh*).

There are quite a few deal breakers!

Lesson 4

Rule #4, Final **y**

WORD BOX

Pattern—Rule #4, Final ***y***: zoological, industrial, secretarial, historically, majestically, happiness, sunnier, slipperier, remedies, penalties, friendliest, sorriest, summarize, apologized, luxuriance, preying, signifying, modification, sprayer, snapper

Directions

Review: Words from lessons 1, 2, and 3.

New words: This week covers a rule from last year: **For final *y* words remember this chant: Change the *y* to *i* after a consonant, except for *-ing* as time has shown. If the *y* is preceded by a vowel then leave it alone.**

If the letter before the *y* is a consonant change the *y* to *i*.

If the letter before the *y* is a vowel leave it alone.

If the suffix is *-ing* always leave the *y* alone.

Rehearse the final ***y*** rule often.

Extra Words

If you are using the extra words, have students practice them on Worksheet B.

- fission
- equilibrium
- fulcrum
- ceremonial
- immediately

Test 4 (45 points)

Heading (3 points)

Spelling Test (1 pt.), full name (1 pt.), date (1 pt.).

Spelling Words (25 points)

Review words are marked with an asterisk.

1. summarize
2. slipperier
3. apologized
4. majestically
5. modification
6. friendliest
7. sprayer
8. signifying
9. sorriest
10. sunnier
11. historically
12. secretarial
13. happiness
14. snapper
15. penalties
16. zoological
17. luxuriance
18. preying
19. remedies
20. industrial
21. snapping*
22. acknowledged*
23. obliged*
24. chieftain*
25. unveiled*

Dictation (17 points)

1. The friendliest one had apologized. (7 pts.)
2. The luxuriance of the king stole our happiness. (10 pts.)

Worksheet 4A

Name: ______________________

Date: ______________________

What is the pattern? ______________________

Repeat and Write (Print)

Alphabetize (Print)

GROUP 1

1. zoological
2. industrial
3. happiness
4. secretarial
5. historically
6. sunnier

GROUP 2

1. summarize
2. luxuriance
3. preying
4. signifying
5. slipperier
6. penalties
7. modification

GROUP 3

1. friendliest
2. sprayer
3. majestically
4. sorriest
5. snapper
6. remedies
7. apologized

Split the Words

Show how each word is made by splitting it into its parts. The first two are done for you.

1. amusement amuse + ment
2. completely complete + ly
3. stylish ________
4. speculated ________
5. definitely ________
6. severely ________
7. fabricating ________
8. navigation ________
9. global ________
10. irritating ________
11. landscaping ________
12. inflation ________
13. fiddler ________
14. insulator ________
15. manipulation ________
16. locating ________
17. generated ________
18. likable ________
19. indication ________
20. argument* ________

Worksheet 4B

Name: ______________________

Date: ______________________

Flip and Write

1. ______
2. ______
3. ______
4. ______
5. ______
6. ______
7. ______
8. ______
9. ______
10. ______
11. ______
12. ______
13. ______
14. ______
15. ______
16. ______
17. ______
18. ______
19. ______
20. ______

Cursive

1. ______
2. ______
3. ______
4. ______
5. ______
6. ______
7. ______
8. ______
9. ______
10. ______
11. ______
12. ______
13. ______
14. ______
15. ______
16. ______
17. ______
18. ______
19. ______
20. ______

Extra Words: Repeat and Write

1. fission ______
2. equilibrium ______
3. fulcrum ______
4. ceremonial ______
5. immediately ______

Alphabetize (Print)

1. ______
2. ______
3. ______
4. ______
5. ______

Review Rule #4, The Final *y*

1. A word that ends with a ***y*** is a final ***y*** word: *beauty, display, busy.* These are not final *y* words: *home, book, pencil.*
2. When joining a suffix to these words observe the following rules:
   - If the letter before the ***y*** is a consonant, change the ***y*** to an ***i***.
   - If the letter before the ***y*** is a vowel, leave it alone.
   - If the suffix is *-ing*, always leave the ***y*** alone.

Lesson 5

Rule #5, **-ness/-ly**

WORD BOX

Pattern—Rule #5, *-ness*:, brazenness, modernness, foreignness, cleanness

Pattern—Rule #5, *-ly*:, willfully, accidentally, critically, sensationally, thankfully, architecturally, agriculturally, psychologically, conventionally, professionally, gradually, occasionally, providentially, fantastically, emotionally, scornfully

Directions

Review: Words from lessons 1, 2, 3, and 4.

New Words: This week covers a rule from last year: **When adding *-ness* to a final *n* word, keep the *n*, when adding *-ly* to a final *l* word, keep the *l* (two, no more).**

When adding the suffix *-ness* to these words keep both *n*'s (*lean* + *ness* = *leanness*).

When adding the suffix *-ly* to these words keep both *l*'s (*full* + *ly* = *fully*).

You will never have more than two *l*'s in any word (*dull* + *ly* = *dully*).

Rehearse the ***-ness/-ly*** rule often.

Extra Words

If you are using the extra words, have students practice them on Worksheet B.

- inertia
- momentum
- office-bearer
- second coming
- campaign

Test 5 (48 points)

Heading (3 points)

Spelling Test (1 pt.), full name (1 pt.), date (1 pt.).

Spelling Words (25 points)

Review words are marked with an asterisk.

1. brazenness
2. psychologically
3. occasionally
4. agriculturally
5. thankfully
6. providentially
7. accidentally
8. foreignness
9. critically
10. architecturally
11. scornfully
12. professionally
13. fantastically
14. emotionally
15. conventionally
16. sensationally
17. modernness
18. gradually
19. cleanness
20. willfully
21. swimmingly*
22. safely*
23. grief*
24. remedies*
25. zoological*

Dictation (20 points)

1. His brazenness had ruined him emotionally and professionally. (10 pts.)
2. No, your modernness is not architecturally useful. (10 pts.)

Worksheet 5A

Name: ______________________

Date: ______________________

What is the pattern? ______________________

Repeat and Write (Print)

Alphabetize (Print)

GROUP 1

1. willfully ______ ○ 1. ______
2. accidentally ______ ○ 2. ______
3. critically ______ ○ 3. ______
4. sensationally ______ ○ 4. ______
5. thankfully ______ ○ 5. ______
6. architecturally ______ ○ 6. ______

GROUP 2

1. agriculturally ______ ○ 1. ______
2. psychologically ______ ○ 2. ______
3. brazenness ______ ○ 3. ______
4. modernness ______ ○ 4. ______
5. conventionally ______ ○ 5. ______
6. professionally ______ ○ 6. ______
7. foreignness ______ ○ 7. ______

GROUP 3

1. gradually ______ ○ 1. ______
2. occasionally ______ ○ 2. ______
3. providentially ______ ○ 3. ______
4. cleanness ______ ○ 4. ______
5. fantastically ______ ○ 5. ______
6. emotionally ______ ○ 6. ______
7. scornfully ______ ○ 7. ______

Worksheet 5B

Name: ____________________

Date: ____________________

Flip and Write

1.
2.
3.
4.
5.
6.
7.
8.
9.
10.
11.
12.
13.
14.
15.
16.
17.
18.
19.
20.

Cursive

1.
2.
3.
4.
5.
6.
7.
8.
9.
10.
11.
12.
13.
14.
15.
16.
17.
18.
19.
20.

Extra Words: Repeat and Write

1. inertia
2. momentum
3. office-bearer
4. second coming
5. campaign

Alphabetize (Print)

1.
2.
3.
4.
5.

Review Rule #5, *-ness/-ly*

1. A word that ends with an ***n*** is a final ***n*** word: *man, green, common.*
   - When adding the suffix ***-ness*** to these words, keep both ***n***'s: *lean* + *ness* = *leanness.*
2. A vowel suffix is a group of letters added to the end of a word that begin with a vowel:
   - When adding the suffix *-ly* to these words, keep both ***l***'s: *full* + *y* = *fully.*
   - You will never have more than two ***l***'s in any word: *dull* + *ly* = *dully.*

Lesson 6

WORD BOX

Pattern—Prefix *uni-*: unicycle, unicorn, unify, uniform

Pattern—Prefix *tri-*: triangle, tricycle, trillion, triplets

Pattern—Prefix *co-*: coauthor, coincide, cooperate, coeducation

Pattern—Prefix *sub-*: submerge, subterranean, subject, submarine

Pattern—Prefix *super-*: superhuman, superimpose, supervisor, superfluous

Directions

Review: Words from lessons 1, 2, 3, 4, and 5.

New words: A prefix is a group of letters that are attached to the front of a word to change its meaning. (The word *pre* means *before*, and *fix* means *attach*.) Most prefixes are from Latin or Greek words, so if you are learning Latin or etymology, be sure to integrate with those topics!

As your students go through these lists, be sure to have them split the words. Hopefully your student will recognize these prefixes on other words.

Extra Words

If you are using the extra words, have students practice them on Worksheet B.

- lubricant
- friction
- resistance
- sovereign
- truce

Test 6 (43 points)

Heading (3 points)

Spelling Test (1 pt.), full name (1 pt.), date (1 pt.).

Spelling Words (25 points)

Review words are marked with an asterisk.

1. superhuman
2. coincide
3. triplets
4. unify
5. superfluous
6. tricycle
7. uniform
8. unicorn
9. submarine
10. coauthor
11. unicycle
12. submerge
13. coeducation
14. superimpose
15. cooperate
16. subject
17. supervisor
18. triangle
19. trillion
20. subterranean
21. mugged*
22. safely*
23. diesel*
24. friendliest*
25. psychologically*

Dictation (15 points)

1. Coeducation is a superfluous subject. (7 pts.)
2. The supervisor and I will cooperate. (8 pts.)

Worksheet 6A

Name: ______________________________

Date: ______________________________

What is the pattern? ______________________________

Repeat and Write (Print)

Alphabetize (Print)

GROUP 1

1. unicycle ____________ 1. ____________
2. unicorn ____________ 2. ____________
3. unify ____________ 3. ____________
4. uniform ____________ 4. ____________
5. triangle ____________ 5. ____________
6. tricycle ____________ 6. ____________

GROUP 2

1. trillion ____________ 1. ____________
2. triplets ____________ 2. ____________
3. coauthor ____________ 3. ____________
4. coincide ____________ 4. ____________
5. cooperate ____________ 5. ____________
6. coeducation ____________ 6. ____________
7. submerge ____________ 7. ____________

GROUP 3

1. subterranean ____________ 1. ____________
2. subject ____________ 2. ____________
3. submarine ____________ 3. ____________
4. superhuman ____________ 4. ____________
5. superimpose ____________ 5. ____________
6. supervisor ____________ 6. ____________
7. superfluous ____________ 7. ____________

Define the Words

A prefix is a group of letters that is attached to the front of a word to change its meaning (*pre* = before, *fix* = attach). Define each word using the dictionary and our simple prefix translation. The first two are done for you.

***uni-* (one)**

1. unicycle *one* wheel
2. unicorn *one* horn
3. unify *one* ____
4. uniform *one* ____

***tri-* (three)**

5. triangle *three* ____
6. tricycle *three* ____
7. trillion *three* ____
8. triplets *three* ____

***co-* (together)**

9. coauthor ____ *together*
10. coincide ____ *together*
11. cooperate ____ *together*
12. coeducation ____ *together*

***sub-* (under)**

13. submerge *under* ____
14. subterranean *under* ____
15. subject *under* ____
16. submarine *under* ____

***super-* (above)**

17. superhuman *above* ____
18. superimpose *above* ____
19. supervisor *above* ____
20. superfluous *above* ____

Worksheet 6B

Name: ______________________

Date: ______________________

Flip and Write

1. ______________________
2. ______________________
3. ______________________
4. ______________________
5. ______________________
6. ______________________
7. ______________________
8. ______________________
9. ______________________
10. ______________________
11. ______________________
12. ______________________
13. ______________________
14. ______________________
15. ______________________
16. ______________________
17. ______________________
18. ______________________
19. ______________________
20. ______________________

Cursive

1. ______________________
2. ______________________
3. ______________________
4. ______________________
5. ______________________
6. ______________________
7. ______________________
8. ______________________
9. ______________________
10. ______________________
11. ______________________
12. ______________________
13. ______________________
14. ______________________
15. ______________________
16. ______________________
17. ______________________
18. ______________________
19. ______________________
20. ______________________

Extra Words: Repeat and Write

1. lubricant ______________________
2. friction ______________________
3. resistance ______________________
4. sovereign ______________________
5. truce ______________________

Alphabetize (Print)

1. ______________________
2. ______________________
3. ______________________
4. ______________________
5. ______________________

Lesson 7

WORD BOX

Pattern—Prefix *ill-*: illegal, illegible, illiterate, illogical

Pattern—Prefix *dis-*: disagree, disqualify, displease, discount

Pattern—Prefix *mon-*: monarch, monogamy, monorail, monk

Pattern—Prefix *multi-*: multicolored, multimillionaire, multitude, multiparous

Pattern—Prefix *omni-*: omnipotent, omnivorous, omniscient, omnipresent

Directions

New Words: This week covers a rule from last year: **For final *y* words remember this chant: Change the *y* to *i* after a consonant, except for *-ing* as time has shown. If the *y* is preceded by a vowel then leave it alone.**

If the letter before the *y* is a consonant change the *y* to *i*.

If the letter before the *y* is a vowel leave it alone.

If the suffix is *-ing* always leave the *y* alone.

Rehearse the final *y* rule often.

Extra Words

If you are using the extra words, have students practice them on Worksheet B.

- velocity
- acceleration
- collision
- Galatia
- throng

Test 7 (44 points)

Heading (3 points)

Spelling Test (1 pt.), full name (1 pt.), date (1 pt.).

Spelling Words (25 points)

Review words are marked with an asterisk.

1. omnivorous
2. omnipotent
3. multiparous
4. monorail
5. disagree
6. omniscient
7. monogamy
8. illiterate
9. multimillionaire
10. disqualify
11. displease
12. illegal
13. monk
14. monarch
15. omnipresent
16. illogical
17. illegible
18. multitude
19. multicolored
20. discount
21. separating*
22. eighth*
23. preying*
24. thankfully*
25. submerge*

Dictation (16 points)

1. The multitude wants to displease our monarch. (9 pts.)
2. The illogical monk was illegible. (7 pts.)

Worksheet 7A

Name: ______________________________

Date: ______________________________

What is the pattern? ______________________________

Repeat and Write (Print)

GROUP 1

1. illegal ______________________
2. illegible ______________________
3. illiterate ______________________
4. illogical ______________________
5. disagree ______________________
6. disqualify ______________________

GROUP 2

1. displease ______________________
2. discount ______________________
3. monarch ______________________
4. monogamy ______________________
5. monorail ______________________
6. monk ______________________
7. multicolored ______________________

GROUP 3

1. multimillionaire ______________________
2. multitude ______________________
3. multiparous ______________________
4. omnipotent ______________________
5. omnivorous ______________________
6. omniscient ______________________
7. omnipresent ______________________

Alphabetize (Print)

GROUP 1

1. ______________________
2. ______________________
3. ______________________
4. ______________________
5. ______________________
6. ______________________

GROUP 2

1. ______________________
2. ______________________
3. ______________________
4. ______________________
5. ______________________
6. ______________________
7. ______________________

GROUP 3

1. ______________________
2. ______________________
3. ______________________
4. ______________________
5. ______________________
6. ______________________
7. ______________________

Define the Words

A prefix is a group of letters that is attached to the front of a word to change its meaning (*pre* = before, *fix* = attach). Define each word using the dictionary and our simple prefix translation. The first two are done for you.

***il-* (not)**

1. illegal *not* legal
2. illegible *not* legible
3. illiterate *not* ________
4. illogical *not* ________

***dis-* (not)**

5. disagree *not* ________
6. disqualify *not* ________
7. displease *not* ________
8. discount *not* ________

***mono-* (one)**

9. monarch *one* ________
10. monogamy *one* ________
11. monorail *one* ________
12. monk *one* ________

***multi-* (many)**

13. multicolored *many* ________
14. multimillionaire *many* ________
15. multitude *many* ________
16. multiparous *many* ________

***omni-* (all)**

17. omnipotent *all* ________
18. omnivorous *all* ________
19. omniscient *all* ________
20. omnipresent *all* ________

Worksheet 7B

Name: ______________________

Date: ______________________

Flip and Write

1. ______
2. ______
3. ______
4. ______
5. ______
6. ______
7. ______
8. ______
9. ______
10. ______
11. ______
12. ______
13. ______
14. ______
15. ______
16. ______
17. ______
18. ______
19. ______
20. ______

Cursive

1. ______
2. ______
3. ______
4. ______
5. ______
6. ______
7. ______
8. ______
9. ______
10. ______
11. ______
12. ______
13. ______
14. ______
15. ______
16. ______
17. ______
18. ______
19. ______
20. ______

Extra Words: Repeat and Write

1. velocity ______
2. acceleration ______
3. collision ______
4. Galatia ______
5. throng ______

Alphabetize (Print)

1. ______
2. ______
3. ______
4. ______
5. ______

Lesson 8

WORD BOX

Pattern—Prefix *semi-*: semiconscious, semicircle, semiannual, semicolon

Pattern—Prefix *para-*: paralegal, paramedic, paratrooper, paraphrase

Pattern—Prefix *ex-*: excommunicate, exalt, exile, exit

Pattern—Prefix *equi-*: equidistant, equator, equilibrium, equation

Pattern—Prefix *du-*: dual, duet, duplex, duplicate

Directions

Review: Any of the words from the previous word boxes.

New words: This week includes more prefixes!

Extra Words

If you are using the extra words, have students practice them on Worksheet B.

- centripetal
- unstable
- divisions
- Corinth
- reek

Test 8 (45 points)

Heading (3 points)

Spelling Test (1 pt.), full name (1 pt.), date (1 pt.).

Spelling Words (25 points)

Review words are marked with an asterisk.

1. duplex
2. exalt
3. semiconscious
4. semicircle
5. paramedic
6. excommunicate
7. dual
8. duplicate
9. paraphrase
10. exile
11. semiannual
12. equilibrium
13. duet
14. paralegal
15. semicolon
16. paratrooper
17. equator
18. equidistant
19. equation
20. exit
21. disbelief*
22. summarize*
23. gradually*
24. submarine*
25. monarch*

Dictation (17 points)

1. The semiconscious paratrooper had made an exit. (9 pts.)
2. The paramedic came into the duplex. (8 pts.)

Worksheet 8A

Name: ____________________

Date: ____________________

What is the pattern? ____________________

Repeat and Write (Print) / Alphabetize (Print)

GROUP 1

1. semiconscious ______ ○ 1. ______
2. semicircle ______ ○ 2. ______
3. semiannual ______ ○ 3. ______
4. semicolon ______ ○ 4. ______
5. paralegal ______ ○ 5. ______
6. paramedic ______ ○ 6. ______

GROUP 2

1. paratrooper ______ ○ 1. ______
2. paraphrase ______ ○ 2. ______
3. excommunicate ______ ○ 3. ______
4. exalt ______ ○ 4. ______
5. exile ______ ○ 5. ______
6. exit ______ ○ 6. ______
7. equidistant ______ ○ 7. ______

GROUP 3

1. equator ______ ○ 1. ______
2. equilibrium ______ ○ 2. ______
3. equation ______ ○ 3. ______
4. dual ______ ○ 4. ______
5. duet ______ ○ 5. ______
6. duplex ______ ○ 6. ______
7. duplicate ______ ○ 7. ______

Define the Words

A prefix is a group of letters that is attached to the front of a word to change its meaning (*pre* = before, *fix* = attach). Define each word using the dictionary and our simple prefix translation. The first two are done for you.

***semi-* (half)**

1. semiconscious *half* conscious
2. semicircle *half* circle
3. semiannual *half*
4. semicolon *half*

***para-* (similar to)**

5. paralegal *similar to*
6. paramedic *similar to*
7. paratrooper *similar to*
8. paraphrase *similar to*

***ex-* (out of)**

9. excommunicate *out of*
10. exalt *out of*
11. exile *out of*
12. exit *out of*

***equi-* (equal)**

13. equidistant *equal*
14. equator *equal*
15. equilibrium *equal*
16. equation *equal*

***du-* (two)**

17. dual *two*
18. duet *two*
19. duplex *two*
20. duplicate *two*

Worksheet 8B

Name: ______________________

Date: ______________________

Flip and Write

1. ______
2. ______
3. ______
4. ______
5. ______
6. ______
7. ______
8. ______
9. ______
10. ______
11. ______
12. ______
13. ______
14. ______
15. ______
16. ______
17. ______
18. ______
19. ______
20. ______

Cursive

1. ______
2. ______
3. ______
4. ______
5. ______
6. ______
7. ______
8. ______
9. ______
10. ______
11. ______
12. ______
13. ______
14. ______
15. ______
16. ______
17. ______
18. ______
19. ______
20. ______

Extra Words: Repeat and Write

1. centripetal ______
2. unstable ______
3. divisions ______
4. Corinth ______
5. reek ______

Alphabetize (Print)

1. ______
2. ______
3. ______
4. ______
5. ______

Lesson 9

WORD BOX

Pattern—Spelling Goblins: vacuum, ache, yacht, awkward, extraordinary, vegetable, all right, weird, column, vengeance, angel, angle, restaurant, possessive, business, receipt, leisure, handsome, parliament, necessary

Directions

Review: Any of the words from the previous word boxes.

New words: This week introduces words that teachers at Logos School have noticed are particularly difficult for students. We call these words "spelling goblins." They are even more difficult than stumpers!

Extra Words

If you are using the extra words, have students practice them on Worksheet B.

- ramp
- liberty
- idolatry
- cram
- carrion

Test 9 (43 points)

Heading (3 points)

Spelling Test (1 pt.), full name (1 pt.), date (1 pt.).

Spelling Words (25 points)

Review words are marked with an asterisk.

1. awkward
2. business
3. necessary
4. vegetable
5. handsome
6. extraordinary
7. yacht
8. vengeance
9. vacuum
10. all right
11. weird
12. leisure
13. column
14. ache
15. receipt
16. parliament
17. angle
18. restaurant
19. angel
20. possessive
21. sprayer*
22. willfully*
23. coauthor*
24. monorail*
25. duet*

Dictation (15 points)

1. The awkward parliament was necessary. (7 pts.)
2. The handsome yacht was for leisure. (8 pts.)

Worksheet 9A

Name: ______________________

Date: ______________________

What is the pattern? ______________________

Repeat and Write (Print)

Alphabetize (Print)

GROUP 1

1. vacuum ______ ◯ 1. ______
2. ache ______ ◯ 2. ______
3. yacht ______ ◯ 3. ______
4. awkward ______ ◯ 4. ______
5. extraordinary ______ ◯ 5. ______
6. vegetable ______ ◯ 6. ______

GROUP 2

1. all right ______ ◯ 1. ______
2. weird ______ ◯ 2. ______
3. column ______ ◯ 3. ______
4. vengeance ______ ◯ 4. ______
5. angel ______ ◯ 5. ______
6. angle ______ ◯ 6. ______
7. restaurant ______ ◯ 7. ______

GROUP 3

1. possessive ______ ◯ 1. ______
2. business ______ ◯ 2. ______
3. receipt ______ ◯ 3. ______
4. leisure ______ ◯ 4. ______
5. handsome ______ ◯ 5. ______
6. parliament ______ ◯ 6. ______
7. necessary ______ ◯ 7. ______

Worksheet 9B

Name: ______________________

Date: ______________________

Flip and Write

1. ______
2. ______
3. ______
4. ______
5. ______
6. ______
7. ______
8. ______
9. ______
10. ______
11. ______
12. ______
13. ______
14. ______
15. ______
16. ______
17. ______
18. ______
19. ______
20. ______

Cursive

1. ______
2. ______
3. ______
4. ______
5. ______
6. ______
7. ______
8. ______
9. ______
10. ______
11. ______
12. ______
13. ______
14. ______
15. ______
16. ______
17. ______
18. ______
19. ______
20. ______

Extra Words: Repeat and Write

1. ramp ______
2. liberty ______
3. idolatry ______
4. cram ______
5. carrion ______

Alphabetize (Print)

1. ______
2. ______
3. ______
4. ______
5. ______

Lesson 10

WORD BOX

Pattern—Stumpers: rhyme, mathematics, quite, quiet, forfeit, grammar, pneumonia, occasion, desperate, schedule, government, library, February, possessive, picnicking, license, enough, chauffeur, counterfeit, laboratory

Directions

Review: Any of the words from the previous word boxes.

New Words: This week has more stumpers. Have fun with them!

Extra Words

If you are using the extra words, have students practice them on Worksheet B.

- symmetrical
- balancing point
- seesaw
- tongues
- variation

Test 10 (46 points)

Heading (3 points)

Spelling Test (1 pt.), full name (1 pt.), date (1 pt.).

Spelling Words (25 points)

Review words are marked with an asterisk.

1. government
2. occasion
3. pneumonia
4. forfeit
5. grammar
6. mathematics
7. picnicking
8. possessive
9. desperate
10. license
11. chauffeur
12. laboratory
13. enough
14. rhyme
15. quite
16. schedule
17. counterfeit
18. library
19. quiet
20. February
21. scornfully*
22. unicorn*
23. illegal*
24. excommunicate*
25. vengeance*

Dictation (18 points)

1. The quiet chauffeur was desperate for a license. (10 pts.)
2. The schedule had grammar and mathematics. (8 pts.)

Worksheet 10A

Name: ______________________

Date: ______________________

What is the pattern? ______________________

Repeat and Write (Print) / Alphabetize (Print)

GROUP 1

Repeat and Write (Print)		Alphabetize (Print)
1. rhyme	______	1. ______
2. mathematics	______	2. ______
3. quite	______	3. ______
4. quiet	______	4. ______
5. forfeit	______	5. ______
6. grammar	______	6. ______

GROUP 2

Repeat and Write (Print)		Alphabetize (Print)
1. pneumonia	______	1. ______
2. occasion	______	2. ______
3. desperate	______	3. ______
4. schedule	______	4. ______
5. government	______	5. ______
6. library	______	6. ______
7. February	______	7. ______

GROUP 3

Repeat and Write (Print)		Alphabetize (Print)
1. possessive	______	1. ______
2. picnicking	______	2. ______
3. license	______	3. ______
4. enough	______	4. ______
5. chauffeur	______	5. ______
6. counterfeit	______	6. ______
7. laboratory	______	7. ______

Worksheet 10B

Name: ______________________

Date: ______________________

Flip and Write

1. ______
2. ______
3. ______
4. ______
5. ______
6. ______
7. ______
8. ______
9. ______
10. ______
11. ______
12. ______
13. ______
14. ______
15. ______
16. ______
17. ______
18. ______
19. ______
20. ______

Cursive

1. ______
2. ______
3. ______
4. ______
5. ______
6. ______
7. ______
8. ______
9. ______
10. ______
11. ______
12. ______
13. ______
14. ______
15. ______
16. ______
17. ______
18. ______
19. ______
20. ______

Extra Words: Repeat and Write

1. symmetrical ______
2. balancing point ______
3. seesaw ______
4. tongues ______
5. variation ______

Alphabetize (Print)

1. ______
2. ______
3. ______
4. ______
5. ______

Lesson 11

WORD BOX

Pattern—Stumpers: capsize, decrease, eject, insubordinate, legible, outstrip, quench, pervade, remnant, swerve, disputations, abnormal, nub, simultaneous, ordain

Directions

Review: Any of the words from the previous word boxes.

New Words: This week has stumpers, which are easier than spelling goblins.

Extra Words

If you are using the extra words, have students practice them on Worksheet B.

- gear
- pulley
- wedge
- firstfruits
- nihilist

Test 11 (44 points)

Heading (3 points)

Spelling Test (1 pt.), full name (1 pt.), date (1 pt.).

Spelling Words (25 points)

Review words are marked with an asterisk.

1. quench
2. disputations
3. ordain
4. onslaught
5. prudent
6. insubordinate
7. legible
8. decrease
9. simultaneous
10. incentive
11. flourish
12. remnant
13. eject
14. catastrophe
15. abnormal
16. pervade
17. capsize
18. outstrip
19. swerve
20. nub
21. superhuman*
22. displease*
23. equation*
24. restaurant*
25. pneumonia*

Dictation (16 points)

1. The catastrophe left only a remnant. (8 pts.)
2. The abnormal disputations began to decrease. (8 pts.)

Worksheet 11A

Name: ______________________

Date: ______________________

What is the pattern? ______________________

Repeat and Write (Print)

GROUP 1

1. capsize
2. decrease
3. eject
4. insubordinate
5. legible
6. outstrip

GROUP 2

1. quench
2. pervade
3. remnant
4. swerve
5. disputations
6. abnormal
7. nub

GROUP 3

1. simultaneous
2. ordain
3. flourish
4. prudent
5. incentive
6. onslaught
7. catastrophe

Alphabetize (Print)

GROUP 1: 1. ____ 2. ____ 3. ____ 4. ____ 5. ____ 6. ____

GROUP 2: 1. ____ 2. ____ 3. ____ 4. ____ 5. ____ 6. ____ 7. ____

GROUP 3: 1. ____ 2. ____ 3. ____ 4. ____ 5. ____ 6. ____ 7. ____

Worksheet 11B

Name: ____________________

Date: ____________________

Flip and Write

1. ____________________
2. ____________________
3. ____________________
4. ____________________
5. ____________________
6. ____________________
7. ____________________
8. ____________________
9. ____________________
10. ____________________
11. ____________________
12. ____________________
13. ____________________
14. ____________________
15. ____________________
16. ____________________
17. ____________________
18. ____________________
19. ____________________
20. ____________________

Cursive

1. ____________________
2. ____________________
3. ____________________
4. ____________________
5. ____________________
6. ____________________
7. ____________________
8. ____________________
9. ____________________
10. ____________________
11. ____________________
12. ____________________
13. ____________________
14. ____________________
15. ____________________
16. ____________________
17. ____________________
18. ____________________
19. ____________________
20. ____________________

Extra Words: Repeat and Write

1. gear ____________________
2. pulley ____________________
3. wedge ____________________
4. firstfruits ____________________
5. nihilist ____________________

Alphabetize (Print)

1. ____________________
2. ____________________
3. ____________________
4. ____________________
5. ____________________

Lesson 12

WORD BOX

Pattern—Stumpers: flounder, canvas, entice, gruesome, melancholy, parch, casual, puny, quibble, regal, stifle, accelerate, vital, downtrodden, ratify, ordeal, erode, bystander, persist, graphic

Directions

Review: Any of the words from the previous word boxes.

New Words: This lesson covers more stumpers.

Extra Words

If you are using the extra words, have students practice them on Worksheet B.

- density
- Archimedes
- Hiero
- heathen
- lubber

Test 12 (46 points)

Heading (3 points)

Spelling Test (1 pt.), full name (1 pt.), date (1 pt.).

Spelling Words (25 points)

Review words are marked with an asterisk.

1. melancholy
2. gruesome
3. puny
4. flounder
5. ordeal
6. graphic
7. stifle
8. parch
9. downtrodden
10. ratify
11. regal
12. entice
13. canvas
14. erode
15. casual
16. persist
17. bystander
18. accelerate
19. vital
20. quibble
21. illogical*
22. paramedic*
23. awkward*
24. forfeit*
25. pervade*

Dictation (18 points)

1. The downtrodden bystander could not persist in the ordeal. (11 pts.)
2. We stifled the puny quibble. (7 pts.)

Worksheet 12A

Name: ____________________

Date: ____________________

What is the pattern? ____________________

Repeat and Write (Print) | **Alphabetize (Print)**

GROUP 1

1. flounder ________ ○ 1. ________
2. canvas ________ ○ 2. ________
3. entice ________ ○ 3. ________
4. gruesome ________ ○ 4. ________
5. melancholy ________ ○ 5. ________
6. parch ________ ○ 6. ________

GROUP 2

1. casual ________ ○ 1. ________
2. puny ________ ○ 2. ________
3. quibble ________ ○ 3. ________
4. regal ________ ○ 4. ________
5. stifle ________ ○ 5. ________
6. accelerate ________ ○ 6. ________
7. vital ________ ○ 7. ________

GROUP 3

1. downtrodden ________ ○ 1. ________
2. ratify ________ ○ 2. ________
3. ordeal ________ ○ 3. ________
4. erode ________ ○ 4. ________
5. bystander ________ ○ 5. ________
6. persist ________ ○ 6. ________
7. graphic ________ ○ 7. ________

Define the Words

A prefix is a group of letters that is attached to the front of a word to change its meaning (*pre* = before, *fix* = attach). Define each word using the dictionary and our simple prefix translation. The first two are done for you.

***inter-* (between)**

1. intermission *between* acts
2. interpret *between* speakers
3. interrupt *between*
4. international *between*

***cent-* (hundred, hundredth)**

5. centimeter *hundredth*
6. century *hundredth*
7. cent *hundred*
8. centigrade *hundredth*

***extra-* (outside)**

9. extrasensory *outside*
10. extracurricular *outside*
11. extraterrestrial *outside*
12. extraordinary *outside*

***hypo-* (under)**

13. hypodermic *under*
14. hypothesis *under*
15. hypochondria *under*
16. hypocrisy *under*

***hyper-* (excessive)**

17. hyperactive *excessive*
18. hyperbole *excessive*
19. hypersonic *excessive*
20. hypercritical *excessive*

Worksheet 12B

Name: ______________________

Date: ______________________

Flip and Write

1. ______
2. ______
3. ______
4. ______
5. ______
6. ______
7. ______
8. ______
9. ______
10. ______
11. ______
12. ______
13. ______
14. ______
15. ______
16. ______
17. ______
18. ______
19. ______
20. ______

Cursive

1. ______
2. ______
3. ______
4. ______
5. ______
6. ______
7. ______
8. ______
9. ______
10. ______
11. ______
12. ______
13. ______
14. ______
15. ______
16. ______
17. ______
18. ______
19. ______
20. ______

Extra Words: Repeat and Write

1. density ______
2. Archimedes ______
3. Hiero ______
4. heathen ______
5. lubber ______

Alphabetize (Print)

1. ______
2. ______
3. ______
4. ______
5. ______

Lesson 13

WORD BOX

Pattern—Science: descendant, scholar, volume, density, physical, suspension, solution, alloy, depose, philosophy, solidify, origins, naturalism, endeavored, ethics, atheism, properties, matter, emulsion, creationism

Directions

Review: Any of the words from the previous word boxes.

New Words: This week includes terms related to debates about science. Hopefully you are going to be covering the issues regarding evolution. If so, these terms should be fun to spell.

Extra Words

If you are using the extra words, have students practice them on Worksheet B.

- Euclid
- mechanics
- engine
- propitiation
- extricate

Test 13 (50 points)

Heading (3 points)

Spelling Test (1 pt.), full name (1 pt.), date (1 pt.).

Spelling Words (25 points)

Review words are marked with an asterisk.

1. naturalism
2. solution
3. physical
4. alloy
5. density
6. endeavored
7. origins
8. emulsion
9. creationism
10. matter
11. descendant
12. properties
13. atheism
14. ethics
15. volume
16. scholar
17. philosophy
18. solidify
19. suspension
20. depose
21. duplicate*
22. handsome*
23. library*
24. remnant*
25. regal*

Dictation (22 points)

1. If naturalism is true, then everything is physical. (11 pts.)
2. The matter began to solidify and its properties changed. (11 pts.)

Worksheet 13A

Name: ______________________

Date: ______________________

What is the pattern? ______________________

Repeat and Write (Print)

Alphabetize (Print)

GROUP 1

1. descendant ______ ○ 1. ______
2. scholar ______ ○ 2. ______
3. volume ______ ○ 3. ______
4. density ______ ○ 4. ______
5. physical ______ ○ 5. ______
6. suspension ______ ○ 6. ______

GROUP 2

1. solution ______ ○ 1. ______
2. alloy ______ ○ 2. ______
3. depose ______ ○ 3. ______
4. philosophy ______ ○ 4. ______
5. solidify ______ ○ 5. ______
6. origins ______ ○ 6. ______
7. naturalism ______ ○ 7. ______

GROUP 3

1. endeavored ______ ○ 1. ______
2. ethics ______ ○ 2. ______
3. atheism ______ ○ 3. ______
4. properties ______ ○ 4. ______
5. matter ______ ○ 5. ______
6. emulsion ______ ○ 6. ______
7. creationism ______ ○ 7. ______

Define the Words

A prefix is a group of letters that is attached to the front of a word to change its meaning (*pre* = before, *fix* = attach). Define each word using the dictionary and our simple prefix translation. The first two are done for you.

***auto-* (self)**

1. autobiography *self* biography
2. automobile *self* moving
3. autonomous *self*
4. automatic *self*

***micro-* (small)**

5. microscope *small*
6. microphone *small*
7. microbiology *small*
8. microfilm *small*

***tele-* (distant)**

9. telephone *distant*
10. telegram *distant*
11. telescope *distant*
12. television *distant*

***pre-* (before)**

13. precaution *before*
14. prefix *before*
15. prejudice *before*
16. prefix *before*

***post-* (after)**

17. postmeridian *after*
18. postlude *after*
19. postgraduate *after*
20. postdiluvian *after*

Worksheet 13B

Name: ____________________

Date: ____________________

Flip and Write

1. ____
2. ____
3. ____
4. ____
5. ____
6. ____
7. ____
8. ____
9. ____
10. ____
11. ____
12. ____
13. ____
14. ____
15. ____
16. ____
17. ____
18. ____
19. ____
20. ____

Cursive

1. ____
2. ____
3. ____
4. ____
5. ____
6. ____
7. ____
8. ____
9. ____
10. ____
11. ____
12. ____
13. ____
14. ____
15. ____
16. ____
17. ____
18. ____
19. ____
20. ____

Extra Words: Repeat and Write

1. Euclid ____
2. mechanics ____
3. engine ____
4. propitiation ____
5. extricate ____

Alphabetize (Print)

1. ____
2. ____
3. ____
4. ____
5. ____

Lesson 14

Review Stumpers

WORD BOX

Pattern—Stumpers: vacuum, yacht, ache, awkward, extraordinary, vegetable, all right, weird, column, vengeance, angel, angle, restaurant, possessive, business, receipt, leisure, handsome, parliament, necessary

Directions

This lesson is a review of the words in Lesson 9.

Extra Words

If you are using the extra words, have students practice them on Worksheet B.

- eureka
- buoyancy
- cosmos
- justification
- doornail

Test 14 (49 points)

Heading (3 points)

Spelling Test (1 pt.), full name (1 pt.), date (1 pt.).

Spelling Words (25 points)

Review words are marked with an asterisk.

1. extraordinary
2. handsome
3. business
4. necessary
5. receipt
6. leisure
7. all right
8. ache
9. yacht
10. column
11. angle
12. parliament
13. angel
14. weird
15. restaurant
16. vengeance
17. awkward
18. possessive
19. vegetable
20. vacuum
21. necessary*
22. occasion*
23. quench*
24. puny*
25. alloy*

Dictation (21 points)

1. The extraordinary angel of the Lord took vengeance on us. (12 pts.)
2. The vegetable gives me a weird ache. (9 pts.)

Worksheet 14A

Name: ______________________

Date: ______________________

What is the pattern? ______________________

Repeat and Write (Print)

Alphabetize (Print)

GROUP 1

1. vacuum
2. yacht
3. ache
4. awkward
5. extraordinary
6. vegetable

1. ______
2. ______
3. ______
4. ______
5. ______
6. ______

GROUP 2

1. all right
2. weird
3. column
4. vengeance
5. angel
6. angle
7. restaurant

1. ______
2. ______
3. ______
4. ______
5. ______
6. ______
7. ______

GROUP 3

1. possessive
2. business
3. receipt
4. leisure
5. handsome
6. parliament
7. necessary

1. ______
2. ______
3. ______
4. ______
5. ______
6. ______
7. ______

Define the Words

A suffix is a group of letters that are attached to the end of a word to change its meaning (*sub* = under, *fix* = attach). Define each word using the dictionary and our simple prefix translation, and then write the list in alphabetical order (print).

-ology **(study of)**

1. geology *study of* the earth
2. biology *study of* life
3. theology *study of* ______
4. cosmology *study of* ______

-rium **(place for)**

5. aquarium *place for* ______
6. terrarium *place for* ______
7. planetarium *place for* ______
8. solarium *place for* ______

-ist **(one who practices)**

9. biologist *one who practices* ______
10. communist *one who practices* ______
11. geologist *one who practices* ______
12. atheist *one who practices* ______

-phobia **(fear of)**

13. claustrophobia *fear of* ______
14. aquaphobia *fear of* ______
15. acrophobia *fear of* ______
16. pyrophobia *fear of* ______

-itis **(inflammation of)**

17. arthritis *inflammation of* ______
18. bronchitis *inflammation of* ______
19. laryngitis *inflammation of* ______
20. tonsilitis *inflammation of* ______

Worksheet 14B

Name: ____________________

Date: ____________________

Flip and Write

1. ____
2. ____
3. ____
4. ____
5. ____
6. ____
7. ____
8. ____
9. ____
10. ____
11. ____
12. ____
13. ____
14. ____
15. ____
16. ____
17. ____
18. ____
19. ____
20. ____

Cursive

1. ____
2. ____
3. ____
4. ____
5. ____
6. ____
7. ____
8. ____
9. ____
10. ____
11. ____
12. ____
13. ____
14. ____
15. ____
16. ____
17. ____
18. ____
19. ____
20. ____

Extra Words: Repeat and Write

1. eureka ____
2. buoyancy ____
3. cosmos ____
4. justification ____
5. doornail ____

Alphabetize (Print)

1. ____
2. ____
3. ____
4. ____
5. ____

Lesson 15

WORD BOX

Pattern—Stumpers: rhyme, mathematics, quite, quiet, forfeit, grammar, pneumonia, occasion, desperate, schedule, government, library, February, possessive, picnicking, license, enough, chauffeur, counterfeit, laboratory

Directions

This lesson is a review of the words in Lesson 10.

Extra Words

If you are using the extra words, have students practice them on Worksheet B.

- pi
- indeterminate
- approximate
- imputation
- catechism

Test 15 Review (46 points)

Heading (3 points)

Spelling Test (1 pt.), full name (1 pt.), date (1 pt.).

Spelling Words (25 points)

Review words are marked with an asterisk.

1. enough
2. license
3. chauffeur
4. quiet
5. picnicking
6. government
7. desperate
8. grammar
9. forfeit
10. occasion
11. library
12. rhyme
13. February
14. mathematics
15. counterfeit
16. schedule
17. laboratory
18. pneumonia
19. possessive
20. quite
21. enough*
22. abnormal*
23. parch*
24. endeavored*
25. parliament*

Dictation (18 points)

1. The chauffeur was possessive of the library. (9 pts.)
2. The government was desperate on that occasion. (9 pts.)

Worksheet 15A

Name: ______________________

Date: ______________________

What is the pattern? ______________________

run + *ing* = *running* but *row* + *ing* = *rowing*

Repeat and Write (Print)

Alphabetize (Print)

GROUP 1

1. rhyme ______ ◯ 1. ______
2. mathematics ______ ◯ 2. ______
3. quite ______ ◯ 3. ______
4. quiet ______ ◯ 4. ______
5. forfeit ______ ◯ 5. ______
6. grammar ______ ◯ 6. ______

GROUP 2

1. pneumonia ______ ◯ 1. ______
2. occasion ______ ◯ 2. ______
3. desperate ______ ◯ 3. ______
4. schedule ______ ◯ 4. ______
5. government ______ ◯ 5. ______
6. library ______ ◯ 6. ______
7. February ______ ◯ 7. ______

GROUP 3

1. possessive ______ ◯ 1. ______
2. picnicking ______ ◯ 2. ______
3. license ______ ◯ 3. ______
4. enough ______ ◯ 4. ______
5. chauffeur ______ ◯ 5. ______
6. counterfeit ______ ◯ 6. ______
7. laboratory ______ ◯ 7. ______

Worksheet 15B

Name: ______________________

Date: ______________________

Flip and Write

1. ______
2. ______
3. ______
4. ______
5. ______
6. ______
7. ______
8. ______
9. ______
10. ______
11. ______
12. ______
13. ______
14. ______
15. ______
16. ______
17. ______
18. ______
19. ______
20. ______

Cursive

1. ______
2. ______
3. ______
4. ______
5. ______
6. ______
7. ______
8. ______
9. ______
10. ______
11. ______
12. ______
13. ______
14. ______
15. ______
16. ______
17. ______
18. ______
19. ______
20. ______

Extra Words: Repeat and Write

1. pi ______
2. indeterminate ______
3. approximate ______
4. imputation ______
5. catechism ______

Alphabetize (Print)

1. ______
2. ______
3. ______
4. ______
5. ______

Lesson 16

Science, American History

WORD BOX

Pattern—Science: scientific, observations, universal, nucleus, membrane, chromosome, cilia

Pattern—American History: industrial, agricultural, constitution, abolitionism, Confederate, Union, articles, mercantilism, economic, tyrant, militia, amendments, secession

Directions

Review: Any of the words from the previous word boxes.

New Words: This week integrates with science and American history, particularly the American Civil War.

Extra Words

If you are using the extra words, have students practice them on Worksheet B.

- hydrofoils
- submarines
- baptism
- penalty
- voracious

Test 16 (48 points)

Heading (3 points)

Spelling Test (1 pt.), full name (1 pt.), date (1 pt.).

Spelling Words (25 points)

Review words are marked with an asterisk.

1. cilia
2. constitution
3. Union
4. chromosome
5. universal
6. observations
7. membrane
8. tyrant
9. amendments
10. nucleus
11. militia
12. scientific
13. Confederate
14. abolitionism
15. secession
16. articles
17. mercantilism
18. agricultural
19. economic
20. industrial
21. swerve*
22. persist*
23. ethics*
24. column*
25. schedule*

Dictation (20 points)

1. The Confederate army wanted secession. (8 pts.)
2. The Union was strong because of their industrial power. (12 pts.)

Worksheet 16A

Name: ______________________

Date: ______________________

What is the pattern? ______________________

love + *ing* = *loving* but *love* + *ly* = *lovely*

Repeat and Write (Print)

Alphabetize (Print)

GROUP 1

1. scientific ______ 1. ______
2. observations ______ 2. ______
3. universal ______ 3. ______
4. nucleus ______ 4. ______
5. membrane ______ 5. ______
6. chromosome ______ 6. ______

GROUP 2

1. cilia ______ 1. ______
2. industrial ______ 2. ______
3. agricultural ______ 3. ______
4. constitution ______ 4. ______
5. abolitionism ______ 5. ______
6. Confederate ______ 6. ______
7. Union ______ 7. ______

GROUP 3

1. articles ______ 1. ______
2. mercantilism ______ 2. ______
3. economic ______ 3. ______
4. tyrant ______ 4. ______
5. militia ______ 5. ______
6. amendments ______ 6. ______
7. secession ______ 7. ______

Worksheet 16B

Name: ____________________

Date: ____________________

Flip and Write

1. ____________________
2. ____________________
3. ____________________
4. ____________________
5. ____________________
6. ____________________
7. ____________________
8. ____________________
9. ____________________
10. ____________________
11. ____________________
12. ____________________
13. ____________________
14. ____________________
15. ____________________
16. ____________________
17. ____________________
18. ____________________
19. ____________________
20. ____________________

Cursive

1. ____________________
2. ____________________
3. ____________________
4. ____________________
5. ____________________
6. ____________________
7. ____________________
8. ____________________
9. ____________________
10. ____________________
11. ____________________
12. ____________________
13. ____________________
14. ____________________
15. ____________________
16. ____________________
17. ____________________
18. ____________________
19. ____________________
20. ____________________

Extra Words: Repeat and Write

1. hydrofoils ____________________
2. submarines ____________________
3. baptism ____________________
4. penalty ____________________
5. voracious ____________________

Alphabetize (Print)

1. ____________________
2. ____________________
3. ____________________
4. ____________________
5. ____________________

Lesson 17

WORD BOX

Pattern—Math: geometric, exponents, opposites, integers, estimating, conversion, probability, circumference, formulas

Pattern—World War II: atomic bomb, corps, Holocaust, Japanese, treaty, mobilization, alliances, infantry, cavalry, trench warfare, camaraderie

Directions

Review: Any of the words from the previous word boxes.

New Words: This week integrates with math and American history, particularly World War II.

Extra Words

If you are using the extra words, have students practice them on Worksheet B.

- Bernoulli's principle
- pitch
- yaw
- instrument
- embassies

Test 17 (48 points)

Heading (3 points)

Spelling Test (1 pt.), full name (1 pt.), date (1 pt.).

Spelling Words (25 points)

Review words are marked with an asterisk.

1. treaty
2. Holocaust
3. cavalry
4. circumference
5. mobilization
6. conversion
7. camaraderie
8. infantry
9. formulas
10. opposites
11. corps
12. estimating
13. geometric
14. atomic bomb
15. probability
16. exponents
17. alliances
18. trench warfare
19. Japanese
20. integers
21. casual*
22. physical*
23. business*
24. desperate*
25. membrane*

Dictation (20 points)

1. The formulas included exponents and integers. (8 pts.)
2. The cavalry will be making a circumference around the infantry. (12 pts.)

Worksheet 17A

Name: ____________________

Date: ____________________

What is the pattern? ____________________

chief but *receive* and *eighty*

Repeat and Write (Print) | **Alphabetize (Print)**

GROUP 1

1. atomic bomb ________ ◯ 1. ________
2. corps ________ ◯ 2. ________
3. Holocaust ________ ◯ 3. ________
4. Japanese ________ ◯ 4. ________
5. treaty ________ ◯ 5. ________
6. mobilization ________ ◯ 6. ________

GROUP 2

1. geometric ________ ◯ 1. ________
2. alliances ________ ◯ 2. ________
3. infantry ________ ◯ 3. ________
4. cavalry ________ ◯ 4. ________
5. trench warfare ________ ◯ 5. ________
6. exponents ________ ◯ 6. ________
7. camaraderie ________ ◯ 7. ________

GROUP 3

1. opposites ________ ◯ 1. ________
2. integers ________ ◯ 2. ________
3. estimating ________ ◯ 3. ________
4. conversion ________ ◯ 4. ________
5. probability ________ ◯ 5. ________
6. circumference ________ ◯ 6. ________
7. formulas ________ ◯ 7. ________

Worksheet 17B

Name: ______________________

Date: ______________________

Flip and Write

1. ______
2. ______
3. ______
4. ______
5. ______
6. ______
7. ______
8. ______
9. ______
10. ______
11. ______
12. ______
13. ______
14. ______
15. ______
16. ______
17. ______
18. ______
19. ______
20. ______

Cursive

1. ______
2. ______
3. ______
4. ______
5. ______
6. ______
7. ______
8. ______
9. ______
10. ______
11. ______
12. ______
13. ______
14. ______
15. ______
16. ______
17. ______
18. ______
19. ______
20. ______

Extra Words: Repeat and Write

1. Bernoulli's principle ______
2. pitch ______
3. yaw ______
4. instrument ______
5. embassies ______

Alphabetize (Print)

1. ______
2. ______
3. ______
4. ______
5. ______

Lesson 18

WORD BOX

Pattern—Science: cellular, manufacture, environment, membrane, diffusion, osmosis, semipermeable, molecule, nucleus

Pattern—Stumpers: abdicated, conspire, authorized, version, subsequent, treason, lapse, paramount, purity, purple, sequence

Directions

Review: Any of the words from the previous word boxes.

New Words: This week integrates with science terms. It has a few stumpers.

Extra Words

If you are using the extra words, have students practice them on Worksheet B.

- combustion
- suspension
- transmission
- mortify
- dexterously

Test 18 (44 points)

Heading (3 points)

Spelling Test (1 pt.), full name (1 pt.), date (1 pt.).

Spelling Words (25 points)

Review words are marked with an asterisk.

1. osmosis
2. manufacture
3. conspire
4. membrane
5. abdicated
6. environment
7. paramount
8. purple
9. purity
10. treason
11. nucleus
12. version
13. sequence
14. cellular
15. lapse
16. diffusion
17. semipermeable
18. authorized
19. molecule
20. subsequent
21. properties*
22. angle*
23. grammar*
24. cilia*
25. integers*

Dictation (16 points)

1. Osmosis allows molecules through the membrane. (8 pts.)
2. Their subsequent treason made us conspire. (8 pts.)

Worksheet 18A

Name: ____________________

Date: ____________________

What is the pattern? ____________________

chief but *receive* and *eighty*

Repeat and Write (Print) **Alphabetize (Print)**

GROUP 1

1. cellular ______ 1. ______
2. manufacture ______ 2. ______
3. environment ______ 3. ______
4. membrane ______ 4. ______
5. diffusion ______ 5. ______
6. osmosis ______ 6. ______

GROUP 2

1. semipermeable ______ 1. ______
2. molecule ______ 2. ______
3. nucleus ______ 3. ______
4. abdicated ______ 4. ______
5. conspire ______ 5. ______
6. authorized ______ 6. ______
7. version ______ 7. ______

GROUP 3

1. subsequent ______ 1. ______
2. treason ______ 2. ______
3. lapse ______ 3. ______
4. paramount ______ 4. ______
5. purity ______ 5. ______
6. purple ______ 6. ______
7. sequence ______ 7. ______

Worksheet 18B

Name: ______________________

Date: ______________________

Flip and Write

1. ______
2. ______
3. ______
4. ______
5. ______
6. ______
7. ______
8. ______
9. ______
10. ______
11. ______
12. ______
13. ______
14. ______
15. ______
16. ______
17. ______
18. ______
19. ______
20. ______

Cursive

1. ______
2. ______
3. ______
4. ______
5. ______
6. ______
7. ______
8. ______
9. ______
10. ______
11. ______
12. ______
13. ______
14. ______
15. ______
16. ______
17. ______
18. ______
19. ______
20. ______

Extra Words: Repeat and Write

1. combustion ______
2. suspension ______
3. transmission ______
4. mortify ______
5. dexterously ______

Alphabetize (Print)

1. ______
2. ______
3. ______
4. ______
5. ______

Lesson 19

WORD BOX

Pattern—Stumpers: notorious, bellow, veto, timidity, beneficiary, lair, surplus, botch, pamper, dilapidated, morbid, lavish, shirk, clutter, parasite, dismantle, farce, futile, grueling, hospitable

Directions

Review: Any of the words from the previous word boxes.

New Words: Another batch of stumpers this week.

Extra Words

If you are using the extra words, have students practice them on Worksheet B.

- frequency
- amplitude
- transverse
- jesting
- thane

Test 19 (46 points)

Heading (3 points)

Spelling Test (1 pt.), full name (1 pt.), date (1 pt.).

Spelling Words (25 points)

Review words are marked with an asterisk.

1. botch
2. pamper
3. beneficiary
4. dismantle
5. shirk
6. lavish
7. morbid
8. veto
9. surplus
10. grueling
11. dilapidated
12. farce
13. clutter
14. parasite
15. futile
16. notorious
17. timidity
18. hospitable
19. bellow
20. lair
21. necessary*
22. occasion*
23. tyrant*
24. trench warfare*
25. purple*

Dictation (18 points)

1. The dilapidated lair had morbid parasites. (8 pts.)
2. The president's veto is a futile farce. (10 pts.)

Worksheet 19A

Name: ____________________

Date: ____________________

What is the pattern? ____________________

Repeat and Write (Print)

GROUP 1

1. notorious
2. bellow
3. veto
4. timidity
5. beneficiary
6. lair

GROUP 2

1. surplus
2. botch
3. pamper
4. dilapidated
5. morbid
6. lavish
7. shirk

GROUP 3

1. clutter
2. parasite
3. dismantle
4. farce
5. futile
6. grueling
7. hospitable

Alphabetize (Print)

Group 1: 1. ____ 2. ____ 3. ____ 4. ____ 5. ____ 6. ____

Group 2: 1. ____ 2. ____ 3. ____ 4. ____ 5. ____ 6. ____ 7. ____

Group 3: 1. ____ 2. ____ 3. ____ 4. ____ 5. ____ 6. ____ 7. ____

Worksheet 19B

Name: ______________________

Date: ______________________

Flip and Write

1. ______
2. ______
3. ______
4. ______
5. ______
6. ______
7. ______
8. ______
9. ______
10. ______
11. ______
12. ______
13. ______
14. ______
15. ______
16. ______
17. ______
18. ______
19. ______
20. ______

Cursive

1. ______
2. ______
3. ______
4. ______
5. ______
6. ______
7. ______
8. ______
9. ______
10. ______
11. ______
12. ______
13. ______
14. ______
15. ______
16. ______
17. ______
18. ______
19. ______
20. ______

Extra Words: Repeat and Write

1. frequency ______
2. amplitude ______
3. transverse ______
4. jesting ______
5. thane ______

Alphabetize (Print)

1. ______
2. ______
3. ______
4. ______
5. ______

Lesson 20

WORD BOX

Pattern—History: engine, combustion, internal, exhaust, crankshaft, valve, friction, kinetic, fluid, shroud, carburetor, lubrication, cylinder, exponent, parentheses, cavalier, Presbyterian, monarch, succinct, tuberculosis

Directions

Review: Any of the words from the previous word boxes.

New Words: This week integrates with more history.

Extra Words

If you are using the extra words, have students practice them on Worksheet B.

- luminous
- translucent
- opaque
- substance
- apparition

Test 20 (47 points)

Heading (3 points)

Spelling Test (1 pt.), full name (1 pt.), date (1 pt.).

Spelling Words (25 points)

Review words are marked with an asterisk.

1. friction
2. combustion
3. Presbyterian
4. carburetor
5. exhaust
6. monarch
7. kinetic
8. exponent
9. internal
10. valve
11. fluid
12. shroud
13. engine
14. tuberculosis
15. crankshaft
16. parentheses
17. cylinder
18. cavalier
19. succinct
20. lubrication
21. quite*
22. economic*
23. conversion*
24. subsequent*
25. grueling*

Dictation (19 points)

1. The combustion in the engine made the cylinder move. (11 pts.)
2. The exponent goes outside the parentheses. (8 pts.)

Name: ____________________

Date: ____________________

What is the pattern? ____________________

Repeat and Write (Print)

GROUP 1

1. engine
2. combustion
3. internal
4. exhaust
5. crankshaft
6. valve

GROUP 2

1. friction
2. kinetic
3. fluid
4. shroud
5. carburetor
6. lubrication
7. cylinder

GROUP 3

1. exponent
2. parentheses
3. cavalier
4. Presbyterian
5. monarch
6. succinct
7. tuberculosis

Alphabetize (Print)

GROUP 1: 1. ___ 2. ___ 3. ___ 4. ___ 5. ___ 6. ___

GROUP 2: 1. ___ 2. ___ 3. ___ 4. ___ 5. ___ 6. ___ 7. ___

GROUP 3: 1. ___ 2. ___ 3. ___ 4. ___ 5. ___ 6. ___ 7. ___

Worksheet 20B

Name: ____________________

Date: ____________________

Flip and Write

1.
2.
3.
4.
5.
6.
7.
8.
9.
10.
11.
12.
13.
14.
15.
16.
17.
18.
19.
20.

Cursive

1.
2.
3.
4.
5.
6.
7.
8.
9.
10.
11.
12.
13.
14.
15.
16.
17.
18.
19.
20.

Extra Words: Repeat and Write

1. luminous
2. translucent
3. opaque
4. substance
5. apparition

Alphabetize (Print)

1.
2.
3.
4.
5.

Lesson 21

WORD BOX

Pattern—Stumpers: dialogue, havoc, innumerable, mull, narrative, lax, adequate, hearth, overture, stalemate, vindictive, implore, emblem, wilt, mar, ajar, infamous, pact, gigantic, misdemeanor

Directions

Review: Any of the words from the previous word boxes.

New words: Another week of stumpers.

Extra Words

If you are using the extra words, have students practice them on Worksheet B.

- diffraction
- incandescence
- luminescence
- edifying
- apothecary

Test 21 (47 points)

Heading (3 points)

Spelling Test (1 pt.), full name (1 pt.), date (1 pt.).

Spelling Words (25 points)

Review words are marked with an asterisk.

1. dialogue
2. stalemate
3. implore
4. misdemeanor
5. wilt
6. ajar
7. innumerable
8. hearth
9. mar
10. infamous
11. narrative
12. havoc
13. mull
14. adequate
15. lax
16. pact
17. gigantic
18. vindictive
19. overture
20. emblem
21. industrial*
22. cavalry*
23. conspire*
24. shirk*
25. succinct*

Dictation (19 points)

1. The stalemate led to an infamous pact. (9 pts.)
2. We implore you to mull over their misdemeanor. (10 pts.)

Worksheet 21A

Name: ____________________

Date: ____________________

What is the pattern? ____________________

Repeat and Write (Print)

GROUP 1

1. dialogue ____________________
2. havoc ____________________
3. innumerable ____________________
4. mull ____________________
5. narrative ____________________
6. lax ____________________

GROUP 2

1. adequate ____________________
2. hearth ____________________
3. overture ____________________
4. stalemate ____________________
5. vindictive ____________________
6. implore ____________________
7. emblem ____________________

GROUP 3

1. wilt ____________________
2. mar ____________________
3. ajar ____________________
4. infamous ____________________
5. pact ____________________
6. gigantic ____________________
7. misdemeanor ____________________

Alphabetize (Print)

GROUP 1

1. ____________________
2. ____________________
3. ____________________
4. ____________________
5. ____________________
6. ____________________

GROUP 2

1. ____________________
2. ____________________
3. ____________________
4. ____________________
5. ____________________
6. ____________________
7. ____________________

GROUP 3

1. ____________________
2. ____________________
3. ____________________
4. ____________________
5. ____________________
6. ____________________
7. ____________________

Worksheet 21B

Name: ______________________

Date: ______________________

Flip and Write

1. ______
2. ______
3. ______
4. ______
5. ______
6. ______
7. ______
8. ______
9. ______
10. ______
11. ______
12. ______
13. ______
14. ______
15. ______
16. ______
17. ______
18. ______
19. ______
20. ______

Cursive

1. ______
2. ______
3. ______
4. ______
5. ______
6. ______
7. ______
8. ______
9. ______
10. ______
11. ______
12. ______
13. ______
14. ______
15. ______
16. ______
17. ______
18. ______
19. ______
20. ______

Extra Words: Repeat and Write

1. diffraction ______
2. incandescence ______
3. luminescence ______
4. edifying ______
5. apothecary ______

Alphabetize (Print)

1. ______
2. ______
3. ______
4. ______
5. ______

Lesson 22

WORD BOX

Pattern—Geometry: integer, regions, fraction, percentage, decimal, classifying, triangles, operations, equilateral, assessment, measure, interior, equivalent, quadrilateral

Pattern—History: treason, subsequent, dictator, economic, tyrant, militia

Directions

Review: Any of the words from the previous word boxes.

New Words: This week integrates with geometry and history

Extra Words

If you are using the extra words, have students practice them on Worksheet B.

- convex
- concave
- periscope
- Melchizedek
- melancholy

Test 22 (46 points)

Heading (3 points)

Spelling Test (1 pt.), full name (1 pt.), date (1 pt.).

Spelling Words (25 points)

Review words are marked with an asterisk.

1. regions
2. quadrilateral
3. treason
4. assessment
5. operations
6. tyrant
7. economic
8. fraction
9. interior
10. subsequent
11. integer
12. equilateral
13. decimal
14. militia
15. triangles
16. percentage
17. measure
18. equivalent
19. dictator
20. classifying
21. alliances*
22. lapse*
23. morbid*
24. valve*
25. emblem*

Dictation (18 points)

1. The equilateral triangles were easy to measure. (9 pts.)
2. The dictator had been an economic tyrant. (9 pts.)

Worksheet 22A

Name: ____________________

Date: ____________________

What is the pattern? ____________________

Repeat and Write (Print)

Alphabetize (Print)

GROUP 1

1. integer
2. regions
3. fraction
4. percentage
5. decimal
6. classifying

GROUP 2

1. triangles
2. operations
3. equilateral
4. assessment
5. measure
6. interior
7. equivalent

GROUP 3

1. quadrilateral
2. treason
3. subsequent
4. dictator
5. economic
6. tyrant
7. militia

Worksheet 22B

Name: ______________________

Date: ______________________

Flip and Write

1.
2.
3.
4.
5.
6.
7.
8.
9.
10.
11.
12.
13.
14.
15.
16.
17.
18.
19.
20.

Cursive

1.
2.
3.
4.
5.
6.
7.
8.
9.
10.
11.
12.
13.
14.
15.
16.
17.
18.
19.
20.

Extra Words: Repeat and Write

1. convex ______
2. concave ______
3. periscope ______
4. Melchizedek ______
5. melancholy ______

Alphabetize (Print)

1.
2.
3.
4.
5.

Lesson 23

WORD BOX

Pattern—Stumpers: braggart, despondent, leisurely, nomad, guilt, rant, seclusion, random, mellow, abound, clarification, embezzle, malady, piecemeal, turmoil, status, heartrending, reimburse, lethargic, cache

Directions

Review: Any of the words from the previous word boxes.

New Words: Yet more stumpers.

Extra Words

If you are using the extra words, have students practice them on Worksheet B.

- Ptolemy
- Aristotle
- pendulum
- priesthood
- sumptuous

Test 23 (45 points)

Heading (3 points)

Spelling Test (1 pt.), full name (1 pt.), date (1 pt.).

Spelling Words (25 points)

Review words are marked with an asterisk.

1. status
2. guilt
3. despondent
4. mellow
5. clarification
6. random
7. leisurely
8. rant
9. piecemeal
10. seclusion
11. braggart
12. cache
13. embezzle
14. turmoil
15. nomad
16. reimburse
17. malady
18. lethargic
19. abound
20. heartrending
21. sequence*
22. surplus*
23. internal*
24. stalemate*
25. percentage*

Dictation (17 points)

1. The despondent nomad ranted about his turmoil. (9 pts.)
2. My malady has made me lethargic. (8 pts.)

Worksheet 23A

Name: ______________________

Date: ______________________

What is the pattern? ______________________

Repeat and Write (Print)

GROUP 1

1. braggart ______
2. despondent ______
3. leisurely ______
4. nomad ______
5. guilt ______
6. rant ______

GROUP 2

1. seclusion ______
2. random ______
3. mellow ______
4. abound ______
5. clarification ______
6. embezzle ______
7. malady ______

GROUP 3

1. piecemeal ______
2. turmoil ______
3. status ______
4. heartrending ______
5. reimburse ______
6. lethargic ______
7. cache ______

Alphabetize (Print)

GROUP 1

1. ______
2. ______
3. ______
4. ______
5. ______
6. ______

GROUP 2

1. ______
2. ______
3. ______
4. ______
5. ______
6. ______
7. ______

GROUP 3

1. ______
2. ______
3. ______
4. ______
5. ______
6. ______
7. ______

Worksheet 23B

Name: ______________________

Date: ______________________

Flip and Write

1. ______
2. ______
3. ______
4. ______
5. ______
6. ______
7. ______
8. ______
9. ______
10. ______
11. ______
12. ______
13. ______
14. ______
15. ______
16. ______
17. ______
18. ______
19. ______
20. ______

Cursive

1. ______
2. ______
3. ______
4. ______
5. ______
6. ______
7. ______
8. ______
9. ______
10. ______
11. ______
12. ______
13. ______
14. ______
15. ______
16. ______
17. ______
18. ______
19. ______
20. ______

Extra Words: Repeat and Write

1. Ptolemy ______
2. Aristotle ______
3. pendulum ______
4. priesthood ______
5. sumptuous ______

Alphabetize (Print)

1. ______
2. ______
3. ______
4. ______
5. ______

Lesson 24

WORD BOX

Pattern—Stumpers: chronological, enchant, foster, hilarious, magnitude, reputable, fluctuate, pall, countenance, ignite, revere, agitation, saga, stodgy, maternal, diminish, grovel, massive, blurt, handicraft

Directions

Review: Any of the words from the previous word boxes.

New Words: The stumpers keep coming.

Extra Words

If you are using the extra words, have students practice them on Worksheet B.

- Copernicus
- Tycho
- Kepler
- mediator
- discoursing

Test 24 (48 points)

Heading (3 points)

Spelling Test (1 pt.), full name (1 pt.), date (1 pt.).

Spelling Words (25 points)

Review words are marked with an asterisk.

1. massive
2. saga
3. hilarious
4. stodgy
5. ignite
6. chronological
7. diminish
8. reputable
9. fluctuate
10. maternal
11. blurt
12. foster
13. handicraft
14. grovel
15. countenance
16. magnitude
17. revere
18. agitation
19. enchant
20. pall
21. farce*
22. exhaust*
23. pact*
24. measure*
25. embezzle*

Dictation (20 points)

1. The stodgy saga is massive and chronological. (10 pts.)
2. We grovel before the magnitude of his handicraft. (10 pts.)

Worksheet 24A

Name: ______________________

Date: ______________________

What is the pattern? ______________________

Repeat and Write (Print)

Alphabetize (Print)

GROUP 1

1. chronological ______ ○ 1. ______
2. enchant ______ ○ 2. ______
3. foster ______ ○ 3. ______
4. hilarious ______ ○ 4. ______
5. magnitude ______ ○ 5. ______
6. reputable ______ ○ 6. ______

GROUP 2

1. fluctuate ______ ○ 1. ______
2. pall ______ ○ 2. ______
3. countenance ______ ○ 3. ______
4. ignite ______ ○ 4. ______
5. revere ______ ○ 5. ______
6. agitation ______ ○ 6. ______
7. saga ______ ○ 7. ______

GROUP 3

1. stodgy ______ ○ 1. ______
2. maternal ______ ○ 2. ______
3. diminish ______ ○ 3. ______
4. grovel ______ ○ 4. ______
5. massive ______ ○ 5. ______
6. blurt ______ ○ 6. ______
7. handicraft ______ ○ 7. ______

Worksheet 24B

Name: ______________________

Date: ______________________

Flip and Write

1. ______
2. ______
3. ______
4. ______
5. ______
6. ______
7. ______
8. ______
9. ______
10. ______
11. ______
12. ______
13. ______
14. ______
15. ______
16. ______
17. ______
18. ______
19. ______
20. ______

Cursive

1. ______
2. ______
3. ______
4. ______
5. ______
6. ______
7. ______
8. ______
9. ______
10. ______
11. ______
12. ______
13. ______
14. ______
15. ______
16. ______
17. ______
18. ______
19. ______
20. ______

Extra Words: Repeat and Write

1. Copernicus ______
2. Tycho ______
3. Kepler ______
4. mediator ______
5. discoursing ______

Alphabetize (Print)

1. ______
2. ______
3. ______
4. ______
5. ______

Lesson 25

WORD BOX

Pattern—Stumpers: cosmopolitan, gaudy, heed, meager, mediate, gala, oppress, imposter, vanquish, affliction, pedestrian, transmit, gratitude, hoax, akin, wan, inflate, impartial, nutritious, elongate

Directions

Review: Any of the words from the previous word boxes.

New Words: A veritable stumper stampede.

Extra Words

If you are using the extra words, have students practice them on Worksheet B.

- Bellarmine
- Barberini
- heliocentric
- revelation
- unrequited

Test 25 (46 points)

Heading (3 points)

Spelling Test (1 pt.), full name (1 pt.), date (1 pt.).

Spelling Words (25 points)

Review words are marked with an asterisk.

1. meager
2. wan
3. oppress
4. inflate
5. gala
6. gaudy
7. impartial
8. gratitude
9. cosmopolitan
10. elongate
11. imposter
12. vanquish
13. transmit
14. hoax
15. pedestrian
16. mediate
17. nutritious
18. heed
19. akin
20. affliction
21. fluid*
22. lax*
23. dictator*
24. mellow*
25. revere*

Dictation (18 points)

1. The cosmopolitan imposter could inflate himself. (8 pts.)
2. The wan and meager pedestrian is in affliction. (10 pts.)

Worksheet 25A

Name: ______________________

Date: ______________________

What is the pattern? ______________________

Repeat and Write (Print) | **Alphabetize (Print)**

GROUP 1

Repeat and Write (Print)		Alphabetize (Print)
1. cosmopolitan	______	1. ______
2. gaudy	______	2. ______
3. heed	______	3. ______
4. meager	______	4. ______
5. mediate	______	5. ______
6. gala	______	6. ______

GROUP 2

Repeat and Write (Print)		Alphabetize (Print)
1. oppress	______	1. ______
2. imposter	______	2. ______
3. vanquish	______	3. ______
4. affliction	______	4. ______
5. pedestrian	______	5. ______
6. transmit	______	6. ______
7. gratitude	______	7. ______

GROUP 3

Repeat and Write (Print)		Alphabetize (Print)
1. hoax	______	1. ______
2. akin	______	2. ______
3. wan	______	3. ______
4. inflate	______	4. ______
5. impartial	______	5. ______
6. nutritious	______	6. ______
7. elongate	______	7. ______

Worksheet 25B

Name: ______________________

Date: ______________________

Flip and Write

1. ______
2. ______
3. ______
4. ______
5. ______
6. ______
7. ______
8. ______
9. ______
10. ______
11. ______
12. ______
13. ______
14. ______
15. ______
16. ______
17. ______
18. ______
19. ______
20. ______

Cursive

1. ______
2. ______
3. ______
4. ______
5. ______
6. ______
7. ______
8. ______
9. ______
10. ______
11. ______
12. ______
13. ______
14. ______
15. ______
16. ______
17. ______
18. ______
19. ______
20. ______

Extra Words: Repeat and Write

1. Copernicus ______
2. Tycho ______
3. Kepler ______
4. mediator ______
5. discoursing ______

Alphabetize (Print)

1. ______
2. ______
3. ______
4. ______
5. ______

Lesson 26

WORD BOX

Pattern—Stumpers: catastrophe, disputations, nub, flourish, abnormal, insubordinate, ordain, prudent, remnant, swerve, outstrip, quench, capsize, incentivize, simultaneous, decrease, pervade, eject, onslaught, legible

Directions

Review: This lesson is a review of the stumpers in Lesson 11.

Extra Words

If you are using the extra words, have students practice them on Worksheet B.

- nebula
- asterism
- elliptical
- martyr
- drought

Test 26 (49 points)

Heading (3 points)

Spelling Test (1 pt.), full name (1 pt.), date (1 pt.).

Spelling Words (25 points)

Review words are marked with an asterisk.

1. catastrophe
2. ordain
3. nub
4. swerve
5. disputations
6. capsize
7. decrease
8. abnormal
9. quench
10. simultaneous
11. incentivize
12. prudent
13. insubordinate
14. pervade
15. remnant
16. onslaught
17. eject
18. flourish
19. outstrip
20. legible
21. havoc*
22. fraction*
23. nomad*
24. hilarious*
25. meager*

Dictation (21 points)

1. The swerve made us eject from the car. (10 pts.)
2. The catastrophe pervaded everything and made the men insubordinate. (11 pts.)

Worksheet 26A

Name: ________________

Date: ________________

What is the pattern? ________________

Repeat and Write (Print) | **Alphabetize (Print)**

GROUP 1

1. catastrophe
2. disputations
3. nub
4. flourish
5. abnormal
6. insubordinate

Alphabetize: 1. 2. 3. 4. 5. 6.

GROUP 2

1. ordain
2. prudent
3. remnant
4. swerve
5. outstrip
6. quench
7. capsize

Alphabetize: 1. 2. 3. 4. 5. 6. 7.

GROUP 3

1. incentivize
2. simultaneous
3. decrease
4. pervade
5. eject
6. onslaught
7. legible

Alphabetize: 1. 2. 3. 4. 5. 6. 7.

Worksheet 26B

Name: ______________________

Date: ______________________

Flip and Write

1. ______
2. ______
3. ______
4. ______
5. ______
6. ______
7. ______
8. ______
9. ______
10. ______
11. ______
12. ______
13. ______
14. ______
15. ______
16. ______
17. ______
18. ______
19. ______
20. ______

Cursive

1. ______
2. ______
3. ______
4. ______
5. ______
6. ______
7. ______
8. ______
9. ______
10. ______
11. ______
12. ______
13. ______
14. ______
15. ______
16. ______
17. ______
18. ______
19. ______
20. ______

Extra Words: Repeat and Write

1. nebula ______
2. asterism ______
3. elliptical ______
4. martyr ______
5. drought ______

Alphabetize (Print)

1. ______
2. ______
3. ______
4. ______
5. ______

Lesson 27

Stumpers Review

WORD BOX

Pattern—Stumpers: rhyme, quite, quiet, forfeit, occasion, desperate, schedule, grammar, government, library, February, possessive, necessary, pneumonia, restaurant, license, chauffeur, mathematics, counterfeit, enough

Directions

Review: This lesson is a review of the stumpers in Lesson 15.

Extra Words

If you are using the extra words, have students practice them on Worksheet B.

- constellation
- Ursa Major
- Babylon
- dholes
- mohwa tree

Test 27 (42 points)

Heading (3 points)

Spelling Test (1 pt.), full name (1 pt.), date (1 pt.).

Spelling Words (25 points)

Review words are marked with an asterisk.

1. government
2. possessive
3. quiet
4. quite
5. schedule
6. license
7. February
8. rhyme
9. chauffeur
10. desperate
11. library
12. necessary
13. restaurant
14. grammar
15. occasion
16. mathematics
17. forfeit
18. counterfeit
19. pneumonia
20. enough
21. decimal*
22. random*
23. grovel*
24. impartial*
25. catastrophe*

Dictation (14 points)

1. The possessive government is desperate. (7 pts.)
2. The counterfeit license was forfeit. (7 pts.)

Worksheet 27A

Name: ______________________

Date: ______________________

What are the patterns? ______________________

Repeat and Write (Print)

GROUP 1

1. rhyme ______
2. quite ______
3. quiet ______
4. forfeit ______
5. occasion ______
6. desperate ______

GROUP 2

1. schedule ______
2. grammar ______
3. government ______
4. library ______
5. February ______
6. possessive ______
7. necessary ______

GROUP 3

1. pneumonia ______
2. restaurant ______
3. license ______
4. chauffeur ______
5. mathematics ______
6. counterfeit ______
7. enough ______

Alphabetize (Print)

Group 1

1. ______
2. ______
3. ______
4. ______
5. ______
6. ______

Group 2

1. ______
2. ______
3. ______
4. ______
5. ______
6. ______
7. ______

Group 3

1. ______
2. ______
3. ______
4. ______
5. ______
6. ______
7. ______

Worksheet 27B

Name: ______________________

Date: ______________________

Flip and Write

1. ______
2. ______
3. ______
4. ______
5. ______
6. ______
7. ______
8. ______
9. ______
10. ______
11. ______
12. ______
13. ______
14. ______
15. ______
16. ______
17. ______
18. ______
19. ______
20. ______

Cursive

1. ______
2. ______
3. ______
4. ______
5. ______
6. ______
7. ______
8. ______
9. ______
10. ______
11. ______
12. ______
13. ______
14. ______
15. ______
16. ______
17. ______
18. ______
19. ______
20. ______

Extra Words: Repeat and Write

1. constellation ______
2. Ursa Major ______
3. Babylon ______
4. dholes ______
5. mohwa tree ______

Alphabetize (Print)

1. ______
2. ______
3. ______
4. ______
5. ______

Lesson 28

Science, History

WORD BOX

Pattern—Science: tissue, digestion, respiratory, accessory, calories, stomach, intestines, mechanical, chemical, metabolism, tuberculosis

Pattern—History: pageant, bequeath, Protestant, villainous, scepter, rapier, usurper, gauntlet, vengeance

Directions

Review: Any of the words from the previous word boxes.

New Words: This week integrates with science and history.

Extra Words

If you are using the extra words, have students practice them on Worksheet B.

- fusion
- asteroid
- comet
- millennium
- warren

Test 28 (46 points)

Heading (3 points)

Spelling Test (1 pt.), full name (1 pt.), date (1 pt.).

Spelling Words (25 points)

Review words are marked with an asterisk.

1. bequeath
2. Protestant
3. metabolism
4. rapier
5. vengeance
6. tissue
7. usurper
8. digestion
9. gauntlet
10. intestines
11. calories
12. respiratory
13. villainous
14. tuberculosis
15. pageant
16. chemical
17. scepter
18. mechanical
19. accessory
20. stomach
21. malady*
22. saga*
23. hoax*
24. decrease*
25. rhyme*

Dictation (18 points)

1. My stomach does a lot of digestion. (9 pts.)
2. The usurper took vengeance with his rapier. (9 pts.)

Worksheet 28A

Name: ____________________
Date: ____________________

What are the patterns? ____________________

Repeat and Write (Print) | **Alphabetize (Print)**

GROUP 1

1. tissue ______ 1. ______
2. digestion ______ 2. ______
3. respiratory ______ 3. ______
4. accessory ______ 4. ______
5. calories ______ 5. ______
6. stomach ______ 6. ______

GROUP 2

1. intestines ______ 1. ______
2. mechanical ______ 2. ______
3. chemical ______ 3. ______
4. metabolism ______ 4. ______
5. pageant ______ 5. ______
6. tuberculosis ______ 6. ______
7. bequeath ______ 7. ______

GROUP 3

1. Protestant ______ 1. ______
2. villainous ______ 2. ______
3. scepter ______ 3. ______
4. rapier ______ 4. ______
5. usurper ______ 5. ______
6. gauntlet ______ 6. ______
7. vengeance ______ 7. ______

Worksheet 28B

Name: ______________________

Date: ______________________

Flip and Write

1. ____
2. ____
3. ____
4. ____
5. ____
6. ____
7. ____
8. ____
9. ____
10. ____
11. ____
12. ____
13. ____
14. ____
15. ____
16. ____
17. ____
18. ____
19. ____
20. ____

Cursive

1. ____
2. ____
3. ____
4. ____
5. ____
6. ____
7. ____
8. ____
9. ____
10. ____
11. ____
12. ____
13. ____
14. ____
15. ____
16. ____
17. ____
18. ____
19. ____
20. ____

Extra Words: Repeat and Write

1. fusion ____
2. asteroid ____
3. comet ____
4. millennium ____
5. warren ____

Alphabetize (Print)

1. ____
2. ____
3. ____
4. ____
5. ____

Lesson 29

WORD BOX

Pattern—Stumpers: accelerate, canvass, erode, melancholy, parch, puny, gruesome, flounder, quibble, ratify, vital, bystander, casual, ordeal, regal, persist, stifle, canvas, downtrodden, entice

Directions

Review: Any of the words from the previous word boxes.

New Words: Back to some new stumpers.

Extra Words

If you are using the extra words, have students practice them on Worksheet B.

- meteoroid
- meteorite
- dwarf planet
- gossamer
- knoll

Test 29 (44 points)

Heading (3 points)

Spelling Test (1 pt.), full name (1 pt.), date (1 pt.).

Spelling Words (25 points)

Review words are marked with an asterisk.

1. parch
2. stifle
3. flounder
4. regal
5. canvass
6. gruesome
7. vital
8. quibble
9. puny
10. downtrodden
11. bystander
12. casual
13. melancholy
14. entice
15. ordeal
16. persist
17. canvas
18. ratify
19. accelerate
20. erode
21. enchant*
22. heed*
23. prudent*
24. possessive*
25. pageant*

Dictation (16 points)

1. The regal lord began to flounder. (8 pts.)
2. The gruesome war persisted and accelerated. (8 pts.)

Worksheet 29A

Name: ______________________

Date: ______________________

What is the pattern? ______________________

Repeat and Write (Print)

GROUP 1

1. accelerate
2. canvass
3. erode
4. melancholy
5. parch
6. puny

GROUP 2

1. gruesome
2. flounder
3. quibble
4. ratify
5. vital
6. bystander
7. casual

GROUP 3

1. ordeal
2. regal
3. persist
4. stifle
5. canvas
6. downtrodden
7. entice

Alphabetize (Print)

Group 1: 1. ____ 2. ____ 3. ____ 4. ____ 5. ____ 6. ____

Group 2: 1. ____ 2. ____ 3. ____ 4. ____ 5. ____ 6. ____ 7. ____

Group 3: 1. ____ 2. ____ 3. ____ 4. ____ 5. ____ 6. ____ 7. ____

Worksheet 29B

Name: ______________________

Date: ______________________

Flip and Write

1. ____
2. ____
3. ____
4. ____
5. ____
6. ____
7. ____
8. ____
9. ____
10. ____
11. ____
12. ____
13. ____
14. ____
15. ____
16. ____
17. ____
18. ____
19. ____
20. ____

Cursive

1. ____
2. ____
3. ____
4. ____
5. ____
6. ____
7. ____
8. ____
9. ____
10. ____
11. ____
12. ____
13. ____
14. ____
15. ____
16. ____
17. ____
18. ____
19. ____
20. ____

Extra Words: Repeat and Write

1. meteoroid ____
2. meteorite ____
3. dwarf ____
4. planet ____
5. gossamer ____

Alphabetize (Print)

1. ____
2. ____
3. ____
4. ____
5. ____

Lesson 30

Science, History

WORD BOX

Pattern—Science: membrane, diffusion, osmosis, cytoplasm, nucleus, chromosomes, organization, protoplasm, cellular, graphic

Pattern—History: translation, conspire, laity, puritan, Protestantism, Catholicism, resplendent, largesse, scourging, abdicated

Directions

Review: Any of the words from the previous word boxes.

New Words: This week integrates with science and history, particularly the Protestant and Catholic conflict.

Extra Words

If you are using the extra words, have students practice them on Worksheet B.

- insulator
- static
- current
- flotsam
- bivouac

Test 30 (49 points)

Heading (3 points)

Spelling Test (1 pt.), full name (1 pt.), date (1 pt.).

Spelling Words (25 points)

Review words are marked with an asterisk.

1. conspire
2. cellular
3. protoplasm
4. chromosomes
5. laity
6. Protestantism
7. puritan
8. graphic
9. organization
10. cytoplasm
11. nucleus
12. membrane
13. osmosis
14. largesse
15. translation
16. scourging
17. Catholicism
18. diffusion
19. abdicated
20. resplendent
21. transmit*
22. eject*
23. necessary*
24. calories*
25. canvass*

Dictation (21 points)

1. The protoplasm makes up the nucleus and cytoplasm. (10 pts.)
2. The Puritan laity have a lot of largesse. (11 pts.)

Worksheet 30A

Name: ____________________

Date: ____________________

What is the pattern? ____________________

Repeat and Write (Print)

Alphabetize (Print)

GROUP 1

1. translation ______ ○ 1. ______
2. conspire ______ ○ 2. ______
3. laity ______ ○ 3. ______
4. puritan ______ ○ 4. ______
5. Protestant ______ ○ 5. ______
6. Catholicism ______ ○ 6. ______

GROUP 2

1. resplendent ______ ○ 1. ______
2. largesse ______ ○ 2. ______
3. scourging ______ ○ 3. ______
4. abdicated ______ ○ 4. ______
5. membrane ______ ○ 5. ______
6. diffusion ______ ○ 6. ______
7. osmosis ______ ○ 7. ______

GROUP 3

1. cytoplasm ______ ○ 1. ______
2. nucleus ______ ○ 2. ______
3. chromosomes ______ ○ 3. ______
4. organization ______ ○ 4. ______
5. protoplasm ______ ○ 5. ______
6. cellular ______ ○ 6. ______
7. graphic ______ ○ 7. ______

Worksheet 30B

Name: __________

Date: __________

Flip and Write

1.
2.
3.
4.
5.
6.
7.
8.
9.
10.
11.
12.
13.
14.
15.
16.
17.
18.
19.
20.

Cursive

1.
2.
3.
4.
5.
6.
7.
8.
9.
10.
11.
12.
13.
14.
15.
16.
17.
18.
19.
20.

Extra Words: Repeat and Write

1. insulator
2. static
3. current
4. flotsam
5. bivouac

Alphabetize (Print)

1.
2.
3.
4.
5.

Lesson 31

WORD BOX

Pattern—Stumpers: chlorine, expanse, copper, demeanor, civilian, conspicuous, devastated, compel, diminished, embodied, conceit, derived, cooperation, contributed, conveyed, contrive, conceivable, counterattack, Colossians, Exodus

Directions

Review: Any of the words from the previous word boxes.

New Words: Back to some new stumpers from a lot of different subjects.

Extra Words

If you are using the extra words, have students practice them on Worksheet B.

- thermoplastics
- polythene
- polystyrene
- hydrophobia
- rabies

Test 31 (45 points)

Heading (3 points)

Spelling Test (1 pt.), full name (1 pt.), date (1 pt.).

Spelling Words (25 points)

Review words are marked with an asterisk.

1. Colossians
2. chlorine
3. Exodus
4. embodied
5. counterattack
6. diminished
7. conveyed
8. copper
9. expanse
10. contributed
11. civilian
12. conceit
13. cooperation
14. conceivable
15. compel
16. derived
17. demeanor
18. contrive
19. devastated
20. conspicuous
21. flourish*
22. library*
23. scepter*
24. gruesome*
25. Protestantism*

Dictation (17 points)

1. The civilians contributed to the counterattack. (8 pts.)
2. His conceit was conspicuous and devastated us. (9 pts.)

Worksheet 31A

Name: ____________________

Date: ____________________

What is the pattern? ____________________

Repeat and Write (Print) | **Alphabetize (Print)**

GROUP 1

1. chlorine ______ ○ 1. ______
2. Exodus ______ ○ 2. ______
3. expanse ______ ○ 3. ______
4. copper ______ ○ 4. ______
5. demeanor ______ ○ 5. ______
6. civilian ______ ○ 6. ______

GROUP 2

1. conspicuous ______ ○ 1. ______
2. devastated ______ ○ 2. ______
3. compel ______ ○ 3. ______
4. diminished ______ ○ 4. ______
5. embodied ______ ○ 5. ______
6. conceit ______ ○ 6. ______
7. derived ______ ○ 7. ______

GROUP 3

1. cooperation ______ ○ 1. ______
2. contributed ______ ○ 2. ______
3. conveyed ______ ○ 3. ______
4. contrive ______ ○ 4. ______
5. conceivable ______ ○ 5. ______
6. counterattack ______ ○ 6. ______
7. Colossians ______ ○ 7. ______

Worksheet 31B

Name: ____________________

Date: ____________________

Flip and Write

1. ____
2. ____
3. ____
4. ____
5. ____
6. ____
7. ____
8. ____
9. ____
10. ____
11. ____
12. ____
13. ____
14. ____
15. ____
16. ____
17. ____
18. ____
19. ____
20. ____

Cursive

1. ____
2. ____
3. ____
4. ____
5. ____
6. ____
7. ____
8. ____
9. ____
10. ____
11. ____
12. ____
13. ____
14. ____
15. ____
16. ____
17. ____
18. ____
19. ____
20. ____

Extra Words: Repeat and Write

1. thermoplastics ____
2. polythene ____
3. polystyrene ____
4. hydrophobia ____
5. rabies ____

Alphabetize (Print)

1. ____
2. ____
3. ____
4. ____
5. ____

Lesson 32

WORD BOX

Pattern—History: castes, aristocrats, serfs, Bastille, bourgeois, edict, financial, Bastille, legislature

Pattern— Stumpers: pathos, apathy, sympathy, pathology, pathetic, dinosaur, tyrannosaurus, automobile, revolution, parameters, encyclopedia

Directions

Review: Any of the words from the previous word boxes.

New Words: This week integrates with history, particularly the French Revolution.

Extra Words

If you are using the extra words, have students practice them on Worksheet B.

- valence electron
- delegation
- contrite
- ardently
- reprieve

Test 32 (50 points)

Heading (3 points)

Spelling Test (1 pt.), full name (1 pt.), date (1 pt.).

Spelling Words (25 points)

Review words are marked with an asterisk.

1. castes
2. tyrannosaurus
3. apathy
4. serfs
5. pathetic
6. sympathy
7. revolution
8. bourgeois
9. Bastille
10. encyclopedia
11. Bastille
12. edict
13. pathos
14. legislature
15. pathology
16. automobile
17. financial
18. dinosaur
19. parameters
20. aristocrats
21. counterfeit*
22. villainous*
23. erode*
24. graphic*
25. expanse*

Dictation (22 points)

1. The castes divided between aristocrats and serfs in strict parameters. (12 pts.)
2. The bourgeois had no sympathy for the revolution. (10 pts.)

Worksheet 32A

Name: ____________________

Date: ____________________

What is the pattern? ____________________

Repeat and Write (Print)

GROUP 1

1. castes
2. aristocrats
3. serfs
4. Bastille
5. bourgeois
6. edict

GROUP 2

1. financial
2. Bastille
3. legislature
4. pathos
5. apathy
6. sympathy
7. pathology

GROUP 3

1. pathetic
2. dinosaur
3. tyrannosaurus
4. automobile
5. revolution
6. parameters
7. encyclopedia

Alphabetize (Print)

GROUP 1: 1. ___ 2. ___ 3. ___ 4. ___ 5. ___ 6. ___

GROUP 2: 1. ___ 2. ___ 3. ___ 4. ___ 5. ___ 6. ___ 7. ___

GROUP 3: 1. ___ 2. ___ 3. ___ 4. ___ 5. ___ 6. ___ 7. ___

Worksheet 32B

Name: ______________________

Date: ______________________

Flip and Write

1.
2.
3.
4.
5.
6.
7.
8.
9.
10.
11.
12.
13.
14.
15.
16.
17.
18.
19.
20.

Cursive

1.
2.
3.
4.
5.
6.
7.
8.
9.
10.
11.
12.
13.
14.
15.
16.
17.
18.
19.
20.

Extra Words: Repeat and Write

1. valence electron
2. delegation
3. contrite
4. ardently
5. reprieve

Alphabetize (Print)

1.
2.
3.
4.
5.

Lesson 33

WORD BOX

Pattern—Stumpers: wrath, amiss, vigilant, detest, salvo, domestic, proficient, flagrant, presume, prior, flaw, fledgling, perjury, fluster, notable, foremost, momentum, paradox, brawl, nurture

Directions

Review: Any of the words from the previous word boxes.

New Words: Another round of stumpers.

Extra Words

If you are using the extra words, have students practice them on Worksheet B.

- iron
- filings
- magnetosphere
- zinc
- domains

Test 33 (46 points)

Heading (3 points)

Spelling Test (1 pt.), full name (1 pt.), date (1 pt.).

Spelling Words (25 points)

Review words are marked with an asterisk.

1. nurture
2. flaw
3. foremost
4. wrath
5. perjury
6. amiss
7. notable
8. fluster
9. presume
10. flagrant
11. vigilant
12. momentum
13. detest
14. brawl
15. prior
16. paradox
17. proficient
18. domestic
19. fledgling
20. salvo
21. usurper*
22. persist*
23. conspire*
24. conspicuous*
25. financial*

Dictation (18 points)

1. I detest his perjury with wrath. (8 pts.)
2. He made a notable salvo into the brawl. (10 pts.)

Name: ____________________

Date: ____________________

What is the pattern? ____________________

Repeat and Write (Print) | **Alphabetize (Print)**

GROUP 1

1. wrath ____ 1. ____
2. amiss ____ 2. ____
3. vigilant ____ 3. ____
4. detest ____ 4. ____
5. salvo ____ 5. ____
6. domestic ____ 6. ____

GROUP 2

1. proficient ____ 1. ____
2. flagrant ____ 2. ____
3. presume ____ 3. ____
4. prior ____ 4. ____
5. flaw ____ 5. ____
6. fledgling ____ 6. ____
7. perjury ____ 7. ____

GROUP 3

1. fluster ____ 1. ____
2. notable ____ 2. ____
3. foremost ____ 3. ____
4. momentum ____ 4. ____
5. paradox ____ 5. ____
6. brawl ____ 6. ____
7. nurture ____ 7. ____

Worksheet 33B

Name: ____________________

Date: ____________________

Flip and Write

1. ____
2. ____
3. ____
4. ____
5. ____
6. ____
7. ____
8. ____
9. ____
10. ____
11. ____
12. ____
13. ____
14. ____
15. ____
16. ____
17. ____
18. ____
19. ____
20. ____

Cursive

1. ____
2. ____
3. ____
4. ____
5. ____
6. ____
7. ____
8. ____
9. ____
10. ____
11. ____
12. ____
13. ____
14. ____
15. ____
16. ____
17. ____
18. ____
19. ____
20. ____

Extra Words: Repeat and Write

1. iron ____
2. filings ____
3. magnetosphere ____
4. zinc ____
5. domains ____

Alphabetize (Print)

1. ____
2. ____
3. ____
4. ____
5. ____

Lesson 34

WORD BOX

Pattern—Review: exalt, semiconscious, dual, semicircle, exile, duet, paralegal, semiannual, duet, duplex, paramedic, semicolon, equidistant, duplicate, exit, paraphrase, equator, equation, equilibrium, semiliterate

Directions

Review: This lesson is a review of the words in Lesson 8.

Extra Words

If you are using the extra words, have students practice them on Worksheet B.

- dipole
- armature
- commutator
- temporary
- motor

Test 34 (44 points)

Heading (3 points)

Spelling Test (1 pt.), full name (1 pt.), date (1 pt.).

Spelling Words (25 points)

Review words are marked with an asterisk.

1. semicolon
2. semiliterate
3. exit
4. duplex
5. paralegal
6. paramedic
7. equation
8. semiannual
9. semicircle
10. duet
11. paraphrase
12. equator
13. equidistant
14. dual
15. exile
16. exalt
17. semiconscious
18. duet
19. duplicate
20. equilibrium
21. ordeal*
22. translation*
23. embodied*
24. financial*
25. proficient*

Dictation (16 points)

1. We sang a duet about exile. (8 pts.)
2. The semiliterate man had to paraphrase. (8 pts.)

Name: ______________________________

Date: ______________________________

What is the pattern? ______________________________

Repeat and Write (Print)

Alphabetize (Print)

GROUP 1

Word	Repeat and Write	Alphabetize
1. exalt	____________	1. ____________
2. semiconscious	____________	2. ____________
3. dual	____________	3. ____________
4. semicircle	____________	4. ____________
5. exile	____________	5. ____________
6. duet	____________	6. ____________

GROUP 2

Word	Repeat and Write	Alphabetize
1. paralegal	____________	1. ____________
2. semiannual	____________	2. ____________
3. duet	____________	3. ____________
4. duplex	____________	4. ____________
5. paramedic	____________	5. ____________
6. semicolon	____________	6. ____________
7. equidistant	____________	7. ____________

GROUP 3

Word	Repeat and Write	Alphabetize
1. duplicate	____________	1. ____________
2. exit	____________	2. ____________
3. paraphrase	____________	3. ____________
4. equator	____________	4. ____________
5. equation	____________	5. ____________
6. equilibrium	____________	6. ____________
7. semiliterate	____________	7. ____________

Worksheet 34B

Name: ____________________

Date: ____________________

Flip and Write

1. ____
2. ____
3. ____
4. ____
5. ____
6. ____
7. ____
8. ____
9. ____
10. ____
11. ____
12. ____
13. ____
14. ____
15. ____
16. ____
17. ____
18. ____
19. ____
20. ____

Cursive

1. ____
2. ____
3. ____
4. ____
5. ____
6. ____
7. ____
8. ____
9. ____
10. ____
11. ____
12. ____
13. ____
14. ____
15. ____
16. ____
17. ____
18. ____
19. ____
20. ____

Extra Words: Repeat and Write

1. dipole ____
2. armature ____
3. commutator ____
4. temporary ____
5. motor ____

Alphabetize (Print)

1. ____
2. ____
3. ____
4. ____
5. ____

Lesson 35

Review

WORD BOX

Pattern—Review: subterranean, unicycle, triangle, coincide, superfluous, submarine, coeducation, unicorn, cooperate, superhuman, superimpose, supervisor, unify, uniform, tricycle, subject, trillion, triplets, submerge, collaboration

Directions

Review: This lesson is a review of the words in Lesson 6.

Extra Words

If you are using the extra words, have students practice them on Worksheet B.

- clast
- deposit
- organic
- metamorphism
- imprint

Test 35 (47 points)

Heading (3 points)

Spelling Test (1 pt.), full name (1 pt.), date (1 pt.).

Spelling Words (25 points)

Review words are marked with an asterisk.

1. superimpose
2. unify
3. supervisor
4. submerge
5. subject
6. superhuman
7. trillion
8. coeducation
9. tricycle
10. uniform
11. unicycle
12. unicorn
13. submarine
14. collaboration
15. superfluous
16. coincide
17. cooperate
18. subterranean
19. triplets
20. triangle
21. cellular*
22. contrive*
23. pathetic*
24. prior*
25. paraphrase*

Dictation (19 points)

1. The triplets cooperate to submerge the submarine. (9 pts.)
2. We had a collaboration with a superhuman unicorn. (10 pts.)

Name: ______________________________

Date: ______________________________

What is the pattern? ______________________________

Repeat and Write (Print) | **Alphabetize (Print)**

GROUP 1

1. subterranean	______	◯	1. ______
2. unicycle	______	◯	2. ______
3. triangle	______	◯	3. ______
4. coincide	______	◯	4. ______
5. superfluous	______	◯	5. ______
6. submarine	______	◯	6. ______

GROUP 2

1. coeducation	______	◯	1. ______
2. unicorn	______	◯	2. ______
3. cooperate	______	◯	3. ______
4. superhuman	______	◯	4. ______
5. superimpose	______	◯	5. ______
6. supervisor	______	◯	6. ______
7. unify	______	◯	7. ______

GROUP 3

1. uniform	______	◯	1. ______
2. tricycle	______	◯	2. ______
3. subject	______	◯	3. ______
4. trillion	______	◯	4. ______
5. triplets	______	◯	5. ______
6. submerge	______	◯	6. ______
7. collaboration	______	◯	7. ______

Worksheet 35B

Name: ____________________

Date: ____________________

Flip and Write

1.
2.
3.
4.
5.
6.
7.
8.
9.
10.
11.
12.
13.
14.
15.
16.
17.
18.
19.
20.

Cursive

1.
2.
3.
4.
5.
6.
7.
8.
9.
10.
11.
12.
13.
14.
15.
16.
17.
18.
19.
20.

Extra Words: Repeat and Write

1. clast
2. deposit
3. organic
4. metamorphism
5. imprint

Alphabetize (Print)

1.
2.
3.
4.
5.

Lesson 36

WORD BOX

Pattern—Science: ethics, philosophy, theology, infinite, finite, presupposition, agnosticism, origins, creationism, theistic evolution, species, evolution, ethical nihilism, naturalism, materialism, atheism, communism, circular reasoning, microevolution, deism

Directions

Review: Any of the words from the previous word boxes.

New Words: This week integrates with evolution again. Add a few more creation-evolution debate terms!

Extra Words

If you are using the extra words, have students practice them on Worksheet B.

- comb
- electroscope
- paperclip
- foil
- hover

Test 36 (44 points)

Heading (3 points)

Spelling Test (1 pt.), full name (1 pt.), date (1 pt.).

Spelling Words (25 points)

Review words are marked with an asterisk.

1. theistic evolution
2. finite
3. communism
4. evolution
5. deism
6. circular reasoning
7. microevolution
8. philosophy
9. agnosticism
10. infinite
11. presupposition
12. naturalism
13. materialism
14. origins
15. ethical nihilism
16. creationism
17. ethics
18. species
19. theology
20. atheism
21. civilian*
22. financial*
23. notable*
24. semicolon*
25. supervisor*

Dictation (16 points)

1. Evolution and communism are false presuppositions. (8 pts.)
2. Naturalism is a species of atheism. (8 pts.)

Worksheet 36A

Name: ______________________

Date: ______________________

What is the pattern? ______________________

Repeat and Write (Print)

Alphabetize (Print)

GROUP 1

1. ethics ______ ◯ 1. ______
2. philosophy ______ ◯ 2. ______
3. theology ______ ◯ 3. ______
4. infinite ______ ◯ 4. ______
5. finite ______ ◯ 5. ______
6. presupposition ______ ◯ 6. ______

GROUP 2

1. agnosticism ______ ◯ 1. ______
2. origins ______ ◯ 2. ______
3. creationism ______ ◯ 3. ______
4. theistic evolution ______ ◯ 4. ______
5. species ______ ◯ 5. ______
6. evolution ______ ◯ 6. ______
7. ethical nihilism ______ ◯ 7. ______

GROUP 3

1. naturalism	______________	◯	1. ______________
2. materialism	______________	◯	2. ______________
3. atheism	______________	◯	3. ______________
4. communism	______________	◯	4. ______________
5. circular reasoning	______________	◯	5. ______________
6. micro-evolution	______________	◯	6. ______________
7. deism	______________	◯	7. ______________

Worksheet 36B

Name: ______________________

Date: ______________________

Flip and Write

1. ______
2. ______
3. ______
4. ______
5. ______
6. ______
7. ______
8. ______
9. ______
10. ______
11. ______
12. ______
13. ______
14. ______
15. ______
16. ______
17. ______
18. ______
19. ______
20. ______

Cursive

1. ______
2. ______
3. ______
4. ______
5. ______
6. ______
7. ______
8. ______
9. ______
10. ______
11. ______
12. ______
13. ______
14. ______
15. ______
16. ______
17. ______
18. ______
19. ______
20. ______

Extra Words: Repeat and Write

1. comb ______ ○
2. electroscope ______ ○
3. paperclip ______ ○
4. foil ______ ○
5. hover ______ ○

Alphabetize (Print)

1. ______
2. ______
3. ______
4. ______
5. ______

Master List of Spelling Words

Lesson 1

Pattern—Rule #1, the Doubler: wrapping, dropping, batting, glowing, splattering, maddening, snapping, saddening, trappings, swimmingly, fittingly, winnable, unflappable, knowable, blower, sowed, sewed, grinned, mugged, slipperiest

Lesson 2

Pattern—Rule #2, Final *e*: safely, sincerely, speculation, immigration, participation, ignition, infiltrator, acknowledged, obligated, negotiated, influenced, irrigating, separating, hesitating, endorsement, amazement, requirement, noticeable, argument, awful

Lesson 3

Pattern—Rule #3, *i* before *e*: feint, spontaneity, unveiled, altarpiece, conceitedly, briefing, neighborly, misconceive, overachieving, grief, chieftain, believability, deceitful, eighth, disbelief, diesel, unwieldy, underweight, counterfeit, height

Lesson 4

Pattern—Rule #4, Final *y*: zoological, industrial, secretarial, historically, majestically, happiness, sunnier, slipperier, remedies, penalties, friendliest, sorriest, summarize, apologized, luxuriance, preying, signifying, modification, sprayer, snapper

Lesson 5

Pattern—Rule #5, *-ness*:, brazenness, modernness, foreignness, cleanness

Pattern—Rule #5, *-ly*:, willfully, accidentally, critically, sensationally, thankfully, architecturally, agriculturally, psychologically, conventionally, professionally, gradually, occasionally, providentially, fantastically, emotionally, scornfully

Lesson 6

Pattern—Prefix *uni-*: unicycle, unicorn, unify, uniform

Pattern—Prefix *tri-*: triangle, tricycle, trillion, triplets

Pattern—Prefix *co-*: coauthor, coincide, cooperate, coeducation

Pattern—Prefix *sub-*: submerge, subterranean, subject, submarine

Pattern—Prefix *super-*: superhuman, superimpose, supervisor, superfluous

Lesson 7

Pattern—Prefix *ill-*: illegal, illegible, illiterate, illogical

Pattern—Prefix *dis-*:, disagree, disqualify, displease, discount

Pattern—Prefix *mon-*:, monarch, monogamy, monorail, monk

Pattern—Prefix *multi-*:, multicolored, multimillionaire, multitude, multiparous

Pattern—Prefix *omni-*:, omnipotent, omnivorous, omniscient, omnipresent

Lesson 8

Pattern—Prefix *semi-*: semiconscious, semicircle, semiannual, semicolon

Pattern—Prefix *para-*: paralegal, paramedic, paratrooper, paraphrase

Pattern—Prefix *ex-*: excommunicate, exalt, exile, exit

Pattern—Prefix *equi-*: equidistant, equator, equilibrium, equation

Pattern—Prefix *du-*: dual, duet, duplex, duplicate

Lesson 9

Pattern—Spelling Goblins: vacuum, ache, yacht, awkward, extraordinary, vegetable, all right, weird, column, vengeance, angel, angle, restaurant, possessive, business, receipt, leisure, handsome, parliament, necessary

Lesson 10

Pattern—Stumpers: rhyme, mathematics, quite, quiet, forfeit, grammar, pneumonia, occasion, desperate, schedule, government, library, February, possessive, picnicking, license, enough, chauffeur, counterfeit, laboratory

Pattern—Rule #5, *-ly*: traditionally, physically, generally, federally, cordially, financially, historically, originally, nationally, mechanically, occasionally, scripturally, distastefully, really, rightfully, mathematically, oily

Lesson 11

Pattern—Stumpers: capsize, decrease, eject, insubordinate, legible, outstrip, quench, pervade, remnant, swerve, disputations, abnormal, nub, simultaneous, ordain

Lesson 12

Pattern—Stumpers: flounder, canvas, entice, gruesome, melancholy, parch, casual, puny, quibble, regal, stifle, accelerate, vital, downtrodden, ratify, ordeal, erode, bystander, persist, graphic

Lesson 13

Pattern—Science: descendant, scholar, volume, density, physical, suspension, solution, alloy, depose, philosophy, solidify, origins, naturalism, endeavored, ethics, atheism, properties, matter, emulsion, creationism

Lesson 14

Pattern—Stumpers: vacuum, yacht, ache, awkward, extraordinary, vegetable, all right, weird, column, vengeance, angel, angle, restaurant, possessive, business, receipt, leisure, handsome, parliament, necessary

Lesson 15

Pattern—Stumpers: rhyme, mathematics, quite, quiet, forfeit, grammar, pneumonia, occasion, desperate, schedule, government, library, February, possessive, picnicking, license, enough, chauffeur, counterfeit, laboratory

Lesson 16

Pattern—Science: scientific, observations, universal, nucleus, membrane, chromosome, cilia

Pattern—American History: industrial, agricultural, constitution, abolitionism, Confederate, Union, articles, mercantilism, economic, tyrant, militia, amendments, secession

Lesson 17

Pattern—Math: geometric, exponents, opposites, integers, estimating, conversion, probability, circumference, formulas

Pattern—World War II: atomic bomb, corps, Holocaust, Japanese, treaty, mobilization, alliances, infantry, cavalry, trench warfare, camaraderie

Lesson 18

Pattern—Science: cellular, manufacture, environment, membrane, diffusion, osmosis, semipermeable, molecule, nucleus

Pattern—Stumpers: abdicated, conspire, authorized, version, subsequent, treason, lapse, paramount, purity, purple, sequence

Lesson 19

Pattern—Stumpers: notorious, bellow, veto, timidity, beneficiary, lair, surplus, botch, pamper, dilapidated, morbid, lavish, shirk, clutter, parasite, dismantle, farce, futile, grueling, hospitable

Lesson 20

Pattern—History: engine, combustion, internal, exhaust, crankshaft, valve, friction, kinetic, fluid, shroud, carburetor, lubrication, cylinder, exponent, parentheses, cavalier, Presbyterian, monarch, succinct, tuberculosis

Lesson 21

Pattern—Stumpers: dialogue, havoc, innumerable, mull, narrative, lax, adequate, hearth, overture, stalemate, vindictive, implore, emblem, wilt, mar, ajar, infamous, pact, gigantic, misdemeanor

Lesson 22

Pattern—Geometry: integer, regions, fraction, percentage, decimal, classifying, triangles, operations, equilateral, assessment, measure, interior, equivalent, quadrilateral

Pattern—History: treason, subsequent, dictator, economic, tyrant, militia

Lesson 23

Pattern—Stumpers: braggart, despondent, leisurely, nomad, guilt, rant, seclusion, random, mellow, abound, clarification, embezzle, malady, piecemeal, turmoil, status, heartrending, reimburse, lethargic, cache

Lesson 24

Pattern—Stumpers: chronological, enchant, foster, hilarious, magnitude, reputable, fluctuate, pall, countenance, ignite, revere, agitation, saga, stodgy, maternal, diminish, grovel, massive, blurt, handicraft

Lesson 25

Pattern—Stumpers: cosmopolitan, gaudy, heed, meager, mediate, gala, oppress, imposter, vanquish, affliction, pedestrian, transmit, gratitude, hoax, akin, wan, inflate, impartial, nutritious, elongate

Lesson 26

Pattern—Stumpers: catastrophe, disputations, nub, flourish, abnormal, insubordinate, ordain, prudent, remnant, swerve, outstrip, quench, capsize, incentivize, simultaneous, decrease, pervade, eject, onslaught, legible

Lesson 27

Pattern—Stumpers: rhyme, quite, quiet, forfeit, occasion, desperate, schedule, grammar, government, library, February, possessive, necessary, pneumonia, restaurant, license, chauffeur, mathematics, counterfeit, enough

Lesson 28

Pattern—Science: tissue, digestion, respiratory, accessory, calories, stomach, intestines, mechanical, chemical, metabolism,

Pattern—History: pageant, tuberculosis, bequeath, Protestant, villainous, scepter, rapier, usurper, gauntlet, vengeance

Lesson 29

Pattern—Stumpers: accelerate, canvass, erode, melancholy, parch, puny, gruesome, flounder, quibble, ratify, vital, bystander, casual, ordeal, regal, persist, stifle, canvas, downtrodden, entice

Lesson 30

Pattern—Science: membrane, diffusion, osmosis, cytoplasm, nucleus, chromosomes, organization, protoplasm, cellular, graphic

Pattern—History: translation, conspire, laity, puritan, Protestantism, Catholicism, resplendent, largesse, scourging, abdicated

Lesson 31

Pattern—Integrated Terms: chlorine, expanse, copper, demeanor, civilian, conspicuous, devastated, compel, diminished, embodied, conceit, derived, cooperation, contributed, conveyed, contrive, conceivable, counterattack, Colossians, Exodus

Lesson 32

Pattern—History: castes, aristocrats, serfs, Bastille, bourgeois, edict, financial, Bastille, legislature

Pattern— Stumpers: pathos, apathy, sympathy, pathology, pathetic, dinosaur, tyrannosaurus, automobile, revolution, parameters, encyclopedia

Lesson 33

Pattern—Stumpers: wrath, amiss, vigilant, detest, salvo, domestic, proficient, flagrant, presume, prior, flaw, fledgling, perjury, fluster, notable, foremost, momentum, paradox, brawl, nurture

Lesson 34

Pattern—Review: exalt, semiconscious, dual, semicircle, exile, duet, paralegal, semiannual, duet, duplex, paramedic, semicolon, equidistant, duplicate, exit, paraphrase, equator, equation, equilibrium, semiliterate

Lesson 35

Pattern—Review: subterranean, unicycle, triangle, coincide, superfluous, submarine, coeducation, unicorn, cooperate, superhuman, superimpose, supervisor, unify, uniform, tricycle, subject, trillion, triplets, submerge, collaboration

Lesson 36

Pattern—Science: ethics, philosophy, theology, infinite, finite, presupposition, agnosticism, origins, creationism, theistic evolution, species, evolution, ethical nihilism, naturalism, materialism, atheism, communism, circular reasoning, microevolution, deism

Master List of Spelling Rules

Rule #1, the Doubler

If you have a single vowel word to add a vowel suffix to, double the lone consonant, but not with ***x*** or ***w***.

- run + er = runner
- row + ing = rowing

Rule #2, Final *e*

For **final *e*** words remember this chant: a vowel suffix drops the ***e***, a consonant suffix can't.

- love + ing + loving
- sure + ly = surely

Rule #3, *i* before *e*

i before ***e*** except after ***c***, or when sounded like ***ā*** as in ***neighbor*** and ***weigh***.

- receive
- eighty

Rule #4, Final *y*

For final ***y*** words remember this chant: Change the ***y*** to ***i*** after a consonant except for ***-ing***, as time has shown. If the ***y*** is preceded by a vowel, then leave it alone.

- plenty + ful = plentiful
- cry + ing = crying
- play + ed = played

Rule #5, *-ness/-ly*

When adding ***-ness*** to a final ***n*** word, keep the ***n***. When adding ***-ly*** to a final ***l*** word, keep the ***l*** (two, no more).

- green + ness = greenness
- final + ly = finally
- dull + ly = dully

Rules for Forming Plurals

1. Add *s* to most nouns to form plurals. Add *es* if the word ends in *s*, *ss*, *sh*, *ch*, *x*, or *zz*.
   - flag flags
   - gas gasses
   - dish dishes
   - ax axes
   - glass glasses
   - match matches

2. To form the plurals of nouns ending with vowel *y*, add *s*.
   - monkey monkeys

3. To form the plurals of nouns ending with consonant *y*, change the *y* to *i* and add *es*.
   - baby babies
   - army armies
   - battery batteries

4. To form the plurals of some nouns ending with *f* or *fe*, change the *f* or *fe* to *v* and add *es*.
   - calf calves
   - knife knives

5. A few nouns change their spellings to make the plural form.
   - child children
   - foot feet
   - man men
   - goose geese

6. A few nouns are spelled the same in the singular and plural forms.
   - sheep
   - moose
   - deer

Name: ______________________

Date: ______________________

What is the pattern? ______________________

Repeat and Write (Print)

Alphabetize (Print)

GROUP 1

1. ______ ○ 1. ______
2. ______ ○ 2. ______
3. ______ ○ 3. ______
4. ______ ○ 4. ______
5. ______ ○ 5. ______
6. ______ ○ 6. ______

GROUP 2

1. ______ ○ 1. ______
2. ______ ○ 2. ______
3. ______ ○ 3. ______
4. ______ ○ 4. ______
5. ______ ○ 5. ______
6. ______ ○ 6. ______
7. ______ ○ 7. ______

GROUP 3

1. ______ ○ 1. ______
2. ______ ○ 2. ______
3. ______ ○ 3. ______
4. ______ ○ 4. ______
5. ______ ○ 5. ______
6. ______ ○ 6. ______
7. ______ ○ 7. ______

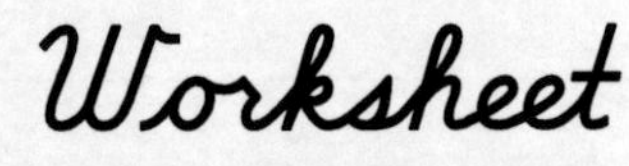

Name: ______________________

Date: ______________________

Flip and Write

1. ______________________
2. ______________________
3. ______________________
4. ______________________
5. ______________________
6. ______________________
7. ______________________
8. ______________________
9. ______________________
10. ______________________
11. ______________________
12. ______________________
13. ______________________
14. ______________________
15. ______________________
16. ______________________
17. ______________________
18. ______________________
19. ______________________
20. ______________________

Cursive

1. ______________________
2. ______________________
3. ______________________
4. ______________________
5. ______________________
6. ______________________
7. ______________________
8. ______________________
9. ______________________
10. ______________________
11. ______________________
12. ______________________
13. ______________________
14. ______________________
15. ______________________
16. ______________________
17. ______________________
18. ______________________
19. ______________________
20. ______________________

Extra Words

1. ______________________
2. ______________________
3. ______________________
4. ______________________
5. ______________________